POEMS OF
BANJO PATERSON
Illustrated by Pro Hart

THE TRAVELLING POST OFFICE
Oil on hardboard 35 x 45 cm 1976

POEMS OF BANJO PATERSON

Illustrated by Pro Hart

NEW HOLLAND

Published by
New Holland Publishers (Australia) Pty Ltd
Sydney • Auckland • London • Cape Town

1/66 Gibbes Street Chatswood NSW 2067 Australia
218 Lake Road Northcote Auckland New Zealand
86 Edgware Road London W2 2EA United Kingdom
80 McKenzie Street Cape Town 8001 South Africa

First published by Lansdowne Press 1982
Reprinted 1983, 1984, 1987, 1988
Reprinted by Weldon Publishing 1991
Reprinted by Ure Smith Press 1992
Reprinted by New Holland Publishers 2007, 2010, 2011

A record of this book is held at the National Library of Australia

9781742571102

Publisher: Fiona Schultz
Publishing Manager: Lliane Clarke
Designer: Emma Gough
Production Manager: Olga Dementiev
Printer: Toppan Leefung Printing (China) Ltd

10 9 8 7 6 5 4 3 2

Contents

Prelude

I have gathered these stories afar
In the wind and the rain,
In the land where the cattle-camps are,
On the edge of the plain.
On the overland routes of the west,
When the watches were long,
I have fashioned in earnest and jest
These fragments of song.

They are just the rude stories one hears
In sadness and mirth,
The records of wandering years—
And scant is their worth.
Though their merits indeed are but slight,
I shall not repine
If they give you one moment's delight,
Old comrades of mine.

Introduction

As the author of the famous ballads *Clancy of the Overflow*, *Waltzing Matilda*, and *The Man from Snowy River*, Andrew Barton ('Banjo') Paterson, has become a symbol of the outback for most Australians. But he managed to cram into an eventful life a great deal more than just writing bush ballads. He was also lawyer, grazier, traveller, journalist, editor, war correspondent, soldier, sportsman, and noted horseman.

Paterson was born on 17th February, 1864 at Narambla, near Orange in New South Wales. During his childhood on his father's property he became an expert horseman and many of his later poems commemorate his love of horse-racing and polo.

He was educated at Sydney Grammar, and during his schooldays lived with his grandmother, Emily Barton, at Gladesville. She wrote poetry and exerted a significant influence over the young Paterson. At sixteen he matriculated and was articled to a Sydney law firm.

Paterson began writing and contributing verse to *The Bulletin* during the late 1880s. He used the pseudonym of 'The Banjo', after a racehorse his father had owned, and his work soon became very popular.

He loved the Australian outback, and combined in verse both action itself and the landscape of action. And there is always in all his writings the laconic humour and fatalistic philosophy of the bushman—constantly faced with drought, heat, flies and dust—yet never going under.

Paterson's poetry belongs to the ballad tradition, the folk poetry passed down to us from the Mediaeval bards. He took the ballad genre and moulded it to fit his songs and stories of the Australian bush. His poems capture exactly the spirit and essence of the people, the vast distances and the harsh and beautiful places of outback Australia.

Through many of his ballads he also became one of Australia's greatest myth makers, not least in *Waltzing Matilda*. His jolly swagman, written to the tune of an old English marching song, has become so symbolic of Australia that it is the nearest thing we have to an indigenous national anthem.

Banjo Paterson was a true folk poet—many of his poems are as much a part of the Australian way of life and tradition as steak and eggs, Bondi Beach and beer. In his lifetime he published several books of verse, two novels, a collection of short stories, a book of memoirs, and the first collection of Australian bush songs. But even more than that, he helped form the Australian heritage and gave city people a glimpse of the beauty and legendary magic of the bush.

Clancy of the Overflow

I HAD written him a letter which I had, for want of better
  Knowledge, sent to where I met him down the Lachlan years ago;
He was shearing when I knew him, so I sent the letter to him,
  Just on spec, addressed as follows, "Clancy, of The Overflow".

And an answer came directed in a writing unexpected
  (And I think the same was written with a thumb-nail dipped
      in tar);
'Twas his shearing mate who wrote it, and *verbatim* I will quote it:
  "Clancy's gone to Queensland droving, and we don't know where
      he are."

· · · · ·

In my wild erratic fancy visions come to me of Clancy
  Gone a-droving "down the Cooper" where the Western drovers go;
As the stock are slowly stringing, Clancy rides behind them singing,
  For the drover's life has pleasures that the townsfolk never know.

And the bush has friends to meet him, and their kindly voices
      greet him
  In the murmur of the breezes and the river on its bars,
And he sees the vision splendid of the sunlit plains extended,
  And at night the wondrous glory of the everlasting stars.

· · · · ·

I am sitting in my dingy little office, where a stingy
  Ray of sunlight struggles feebly down between the houses tall,
And the foetid air and gritty of the dusty, dirty city,
  Through the open window floating, spreads its foulness over all.

And in place of lowing cattle, I can hear the fiendish rattle
  Of the tramways and the buses making hurry down the street;
And the language uninviting of the gutter children fighting
  Comes fitfully and faintly through the ceaseless tramp of feet.

And the hurrying people daunt me, and their pallid faces haunt me
  As they shoulder one another in their rush and nervous haste,
With their eager eyes and greedy, and their stunted forms and
      weedy,
  For townsfolk have no time to grow, they have no time to waste.

And I somehow rather fancy that I'd like to change with Clancy,
  Like to take a turn at droving where the seasons come and go,
While he faced the round eternal of the cash-book and the journal—
  But I doubt he'd suit the office, Clancy, of The Overflow.

CLANCY OF THE OVERFLOW
Oil on canvas board 18in. × 14in. 1974

Geebung Polo Club

It was somewhere up the country, in a land of rock and scrub,
That they formed an institution called the Geebung Polo Club.
They were long and wiry natives from the rugged mountain side,
And the horse was never saddled that the Geebungs couldn't ride;
But their style of playing polo was irregular and rash—
They had mighty little science, but a mighty lot of dash:
And they played on mountain ponies that were muscular and
    strong,
Though their coats were quite unpolished, and their manes and tails
    were long.
And they used to train those ponies wheeling cattle in the scrub;
They were demons, were the members of the Geebung Polo Club.

It was somewhere down the country, in a city's smoke and steam,
That a polo club existed, called "The Cuff and Collar Team".
As a social institution 'twas a marvellous success,
For the members were distinguished by exclusiveness and dress.
They had natty little ponies that were nice, and smooth, and sleek,
For their cultivated owners only rode 'em once a week.
So they started up the country in pursuit of sport and fame,
For they meant to show the Geebungs how they ought to play
    the game;
And they took their valets with them—just to give their boots a rub
Ere they started operations on the Geebung Polo Club.

Now my readers can imagine how the contest ebbed and flowed,
When the Geebung boys got going it was time to clear the road;
And the game was so terrific that ere half the time was gone
A spectator's leg was broken—just from merely looking on.
For they waddied one another till the plain was strewn with dead,
While the score was kept so even that they neither got ahead.
And the Cuff and Collar Captain, when he tumbled off to die
Was the last surviving player—so the game was called a tie.
Then the Captain of the Geebungs raised him slowly from the
    ground,
Though his wounds were mostly mortal, yet he fiercely gazed
    around;
There was no one to oppose him—all the rest were in a trance,
So he scrambled on his pony for his last expiring chance,
For he meant to make an effort to get victory to his side;
So he struck at goal—and missed it—then he tumbled off and died.

· · · · · · ·

By the old Campaspe River, where the breezes shake the grass,
There's a row of little gravestones that the stockmen never pass,
For they bear a rude inscription saying, "Stranger, drop a tear,
For the Cuff and Collar players and the Geebung boys lie here."
And on misty moonlit evenings, while the dingoes howl around,
You can see their shadows flitting down that phantom polo ground;
You can hear the loud collisions as the flying players meet,
And the rattle of the mallets, and the rush of ponies' feet,
Till the terrified spectator rides like blazes to the pub—
He's been haunted by the spectres of the Geebung Polo Club.

GEEBUNG POLO CLUB
Oil on canvas board 18in. × 14in. 1974

Lost

"HE ought to be home," said the old man. "without there's something amiss.
He only went to the Two-mile—he ought to be back by this.
He *would* ride the Reckless filly, he *would* have his wilful way;
And here, he's not back at sundown—and what will his mother say?

"He was always his mother's idol, since ever his father died;
And there isn't a horse on the station that he isn't game to ride.
But that Reckless mare is vicious, and if once she gets away
He hasn't got strength to hold her—and what will his mother say?"

The old man walked to the sliprail, and peered up the darkening track,
And looked and longed for the rider that would never more come back;
And the mother came and clutched him, with sudden, spasmodic fright:
"What has become of my Willie?—why isn't he home tonight?"

Away in the gloomy ranges, at the foot of an ironbark,
The bonnie, winsome laddie was lying stiff and stark;
For the Reckless mare had smashed him against a leaning limb,
And his comely face was battered, and his merry eyes were dim.

And the thoroughbred chestnut filly, the saddle beneath her flanks,
Was away like fire through the ranges to join the wild mob's ranks;
And a broken-hearted woman and an old man worn and white
Were searching all day in the ranges till the sundown brought the night.

And the mother kept feebly calling, with a hope that would not die,
"Willie! where are you, Willie?" But how can the dead reply?
And hope died out with the daylight, and the darkness brought despair.
God pity the stricken mother, and answer the widow's prayer!

Though far and wide they sought him, they found not where he fell;
For the ranges held him precious, and guarded their treasure well.
The wattle blooms above him, and the blue bells blow close by,
And the brown bees buzz the secret, and the wild birds sing reply.

LOST
Oil on canvas board 18in. × 14in. 1974

But the mother pined and faded, and cried, and took no rest,
And rode each day to the ranges on her hopeless, weary quest,
Seeking her loved one ever, she faded and pined away,
But with strength of her great affection she still sought every day.

"I know that sooner or later I shall find my boy," she said.
But she came not home one evening, and they found her lying dead,
And stamped on the poor pale features, as the spirit homeward
    passed,
Was an angel smile of gladness—she had found her boy at last.

The Man From Snowy River

THERE was movement at the station, for the word had passed
    around
  That the colt from old Regret had got away,
And had joined the wild bush horses—he was worth a thousand
    pound,
  So all the cracks had gathered to the fray.
All the tried and noted riders from the stations near and far
  Had mustered at the homestead overnight,
For the bushmen love hard riding where the wild bush horses are,
  And the stock-horse snuffs the battle with delight.

There was Harrison, who made his pile when Pardon won the cup,
  The old man with his hair as white as snow;
But few could ride beside him when his blood was fairly up—
  He would go wherever horse and man could go.
And Clancy of the Overflow came down to lend a hand,
  No better horseman ever held the reins;
For never horse could throw him while the saddle-girths would
    stand—
  He learnt to ride while droving on the plains.

And one was there, a stripling on a small and weedy beast;
  He was something like a racehorse undersized,
With a touch of Timor pony—three parts thoroughbred at least—
  And such as are by mountain horsemen prized.
He was hard and tough and wiry—just the sort that won't say die—
  There was courage in his quick impatient tread;
And he bore the badge of gameness in his bright and fiery eye,
  And the proud and lofty carriage of his head.

But still so slight and weedy, one would doubt his power to stay,
  And the old man said, "That horse will never do
For a long and tiring gallop—lad, you'd better stop away,
  Those hills are far too rough for such as you."
So he waited, sad and wistful—only Clancy stood his friend—
  "I think we ought to let him come," he said:
"I warrant he'll be with us when he's wanted at the end,
  For both his horse and he are mountain bred.

"He hails from Snowy River, up by Kosciusko's side,
  Where the hills are twice as steep and twice as rough;
Where a horse's hoofs strike firelight from the flint stones every
    stride,
  The man that holds his own is good enough.
And the Snowy River riders on the mountains make their home,
  Where the river runs those giant hills between;
I have seen full many horsemen since I first commenced to roam,
But nowhere yet such horsemen have I seen."

So he went; they found the horses by the big mimosa clump,
    They raced away towards the mountain's brow,
And the old man gave his orders, "Boys, go at them from the jump,
    No use to try for fancy riding now.
And, Clancy, you must wheel them, try and wheel them to the right.
    Ride boldly, lad, and never fear the spills,
For never yet was rider that could keep the mob in sight,
    If once they gain the shelter of those hills."

So Clancy rode to wheel them—he was racing on the wing
    Where the best and boldest riders take their place,
And he raced his stock-horse past them, and he made the ranges ring
    With the stockwhip, as he met them face to face.
Then they halted for a moment, while he swung the dreaded lash,
    But they saw their well-loved mountain full in view,
And they charged beneath the stockwhip with a sharp and sudden
      dash,
    And off into the mountain scrub they flew.

Then fast the horsemen followed, where the gorges deep and black
    Resounded to the thunder of their tread,
And the stockwhips woke the echoes, and they fiercely answered
      back
    From cliffs and crags that beetled overhead.
And upward, ever upward, the wild horses held their way,
    Where mountain ash and kurrajong grew wide;
And the old man muttered fiercely, "We may bid the mob good day,
    No man can hold them down the other side."

When they reached the mountain's summit, even Clancy took a
      pull—
    It well might make the boldest hold their breath;
The wild hop scrub grew thickly, and the hidden ground was full
    Of wombat holes, and any slip was death.

But the man from Snowy River let the pony have his head,
    And he swung his stockwhip round and gave a cheer,
And he raced him down the mountain like a torrent down its bed,
    While the others stood and watched in very fear.

He sent the flint-stones flying, but the pony kept his feet,
    He cleared the fallen timber in his stride,
And the man from Snowy River never shifted in his seat—
    It was grand to see that mountain horseman ride.
Through the stringy barks and saplings, on the rough and broken
      ground,
    Down the hillside at a racing pace he went;
And he never drew the bridle till he landed safe and sound
    At the bottom of that terrible descent.

THE MAN FROM SNOWY RIVER
Oil on canvas board 18in. × 14in. 1974

He was right among the horses as they climbed the farther hill,
    And the watchers on the mountain, standing mute,
Saw him ply the stockwhip fiercely; he was right among them still,
    As he raced across the clearing in pursuit.
Then they lost him for a moment, where two mountain gullies met
    In the ranges—but a final glimpse reveals
On a dim and distant hillside the wild horses racing yet,
    With the man from Snowy River at their heels.

And he ran them single-handed till their sides were white with foam;
    He followed like a bloodhound on their track,
Till they halted, cowed and beaten; then he turned their heads for
        home,
    And alone and unassisted brought them back.
But his hardy mountain pony he could scarcely raise a trot,
    He was blood from hip to shoulder from the spur;
But his pluck was still undaunted, and his courage fiery hot,
    For never yet was mountain horse a cur.

And down by Kosciusko, where the pine-clad ridges raise
    Their torn and rugged battlements on high,
Where the air is clear as crystal, and the white stars fairly blaze
    At midnight in the cold and frosty sky,
And where around the Overflow the reed-beds sweep and sway
    To the breezes, and the rolling plains are wide,
The Man from Snowy River is a household word today,
    And the stockmen tell the story of his ride.

THE MAN FROM SNOWY RIVER
Oil on canvas board 18in. × 14in. 1974

The Swagman's Rest

We buried old Bob where the bloodwoods wave
  At the foot of the Eaglehawk;
We fashioned a cross on the old man's grave
  For fear that his ghost might walk;
We carved his name on a bloodwood tree
  With the date of his sad decease
And in place of "Died from effects of spree"
  We wrote "May he rest in peace".

For Bob was known on the Overland,
  A regular old bush wag,
Tramping along in the dust and sand,
  Humping his well-worn swag.
He would camp for days in the river-bed,
  And loiter and "fish for whales".
"I'm into the swagman's yard," he said.
  "And I never shall find the rails."

But he found the rails on that summer night
  For a better place—or worse,
As we watched by turns in the flickering light
  With an old black gin for nurse.
The breeze came in with the scent of pine,
  The river sounded clear,
When a change came on, and we saw the sign
  That told us the end was near.

He spoke in a cultured voice and low—
  "I fancy they've 'sent the route';
I once was an army man, you know.
  Though now I'm a drunken brute;
But bury me out where the bloodwoods wave,
  And, if ever you're fairly stuck,
Just take and shovel me out of the grave
  And, maybe, I'll bring you luck.

THE SWAGMAN'S REST
Oil on hardboard 18in. × 14in. 1974

"For I've always heard—" here his voice grew weak,
  His strength was wellnigh sped,
He gasped and struggled and tried to speak,
  Then fell in a moment—dead.
Thus ended a wasted life and hard,
  Of energies misapplied—
Old Bob was out of the "swagman's yard"
  And over the Great Divide.

.   .   .   .   .

The drought came down on the field and flock,
  And never a raindrop fell,
Though the tortured moans of the starving stock
  Might soften a fiend from hell.
And we thought of the hint that the swagman gave
  When he went to the Great Unseen—
We shovelled the skeleton out of the grave
  To see what his hint might mean.

We dug where the cross and the grave posts were,
  We shovelled away the mould,
When sudden a vein of quartz lay bare
  All gleaming with yellow gold.
'Twas a reef with never a fault nor baulk
  That ran from the range's crest,
And the richest mine on the Eaglehawk
  Is known as "The Swagman's Rest".

The Road to Hogan's Gap

Now look, you see, it's this way like—
  You cross the broken bridge
And run the crick down, till you strike
  The second right-hand ridge.

The track is hard to see in parts,
  But still it's pretty clear;
There's been two Injun hawkers' carts
  Along that road this year.

Well, run that right-hand ridge along—
  It ain't, to say, too steep—
There's two fresh tracks might put you wrong
  Where blokes went out with sheep.

But keep the crick upon your right,
  And follow pretty straight
Along the spur, until you sight
  A wire and sapling gate.

Well, that's where Hogan's old grey mare
  Fell off and broke her back;
You'll see her carcass layin' there,
  Jist down below the track.

And then you drop two mile, or three,
  It's pretty steep and blind;
You want to go and fall a tree
  And tie it on behind.

And then you pass a broken cart
  Below a granite bluff;
And that is where you strike the part
  They reckon pretty rough.

But by the time you've got that far
  It's either cure or kill,
So turn your horses round the spur
  And face 'em up the hill.

For look, if you should miss the slope
  And get below the track,
You haven't got the slightest hope
  Of ever gettin' back.

An' half way up you'll see the hide
  Of Hogan's brindled bull;
Well, mind and keep the right-hand side.
  The left's too steep a pull.

And both the banks is full of cracks;
　　An' just about at dark
You'll see the last year's bullock tracks
　　Where Hogan drew the bark.

The marks is old and pretty faint—
　　O'ergrown with scrub and such;
Of course the track to Hogan's ain't
　　A road that's travelled much.

But turn and run the tracks along
　　For half a mile or more,
And then, of course, you can't go wrong—
　　You're right at Hogan's door.

When first you come to Hogan's gate
　　He mightn't show perhaps;
He's pretty sure to plant, and wait
　　To see it ain't the traps.

I wouldn't call it good enough
　　To let your horses out;
There's some that's pretty extra rough
　　Is livin' round about.

It's likely, if your horses did
　　Get feedin' near the track
It's going to cost at least a quid
　　Or more to get them back.

So, if you find they're off the place,
　　It's up to you to go
And flash a quid in Hogan's face—
　　He'll know the blokes that know.

But listen—if you're feelin' dry,
　　Just see there's no one near,
And go and wink the other eye
　　And ask for ginger beer.

The blokes come in from near and far
　　To sample Hogan's pop;
They reckon once they breast the bar
　　They stay there till they drop.

On Sundays you can see them spread
　　Like flies around the tap.
It's like that song "The Livin' Dead"
　　Up there at Hogan's Gap.

THE ROAD TO HOGAN'S GAP
Oil on hardboard 18in. × 14in. 1974

They like to make it pretty strong
  Whenever there's a chance;
So when a stranger comes along
  They always hold a dance.

There's recitations, songs, and fights—
  A willin' lot you'll meet.
There's one long bloke up there recites;
  I tell you he's a treat.

They're lively blokes all right up there,
  It's never dull a day.
I'd go meself if I could spare
  The time to get away.

      .   .   .   .   .   .

The stranger turned his horses quick.
  He didn't cross the bridge;
He didn't go along the crick
  To strike the second ridge;

He didn't make the trip, because
  He wasn't feeling fit.
His business up at Hogan's was
  To serve him with a writ.

He reckoned, if he faced the pull
  And climbed the rocky stair,
The next to come might find his hide
A landmark on the mountain side,
Along with Hogan's brindled bull
  And Hogan's old grey mare!

THE ROAD TO HOGAN'S GAP
Oil on canvas board 16in. × 13½in. 1974

Song of the Wheat

WE have sung the song of the droving days,
  Of the march of the travelling sheep—
How by silent stages and lonely ways
  Thin, white battalions creep.
But the man who now by the land would thrive
  Must his spurs to a ploughshare beat;
And the bush bard, changing his tune, may strive
  To sing the song of the Wheat!

It's west by south of the Great Divide
  The grim grey plains run out,
Where the old flock-masters lived and died
  In a ceaseless fight with drought.
Weary with waiting and hope deferred
  They were ready to own defeat,
Till at last they heard the master-word—
  And the master-word was Wheat.

Yarran and Myall and Box and Pine—
  'Twas axe and fire for all;
They scarce could tarry to blaze the line
  Or wait for the trees to fall
Ere the team was yoked, and the gates flung wide,
  And the dust of the horses' feet
Rose up like a pillar of smoke to guide
  The wonderful march of Wheat.

Furrow by furrow, and fold by fold,
  The soil is turned on the plain;
Better than silver and better than gold
  Is the surface-mine of the grain.
Better than cattle and better than sheep
  In the fight with drought and heat;
For a streak of stubbornness, wide and deep,
  Lies hid in a grain of Wheat.

When the stock is swept by the hand of fate,
  Deep down on his bed of clay
The brave brown Wheat will die and wait
  For the resurrection day—
Lie hid while the whole world thinks him dead;
  But the Spring-rain, soft and sweet,
Will over the steaming paddocks spread ·
  The first green flush of the Wheat.

SONG OF THE WHEAT
Oil on hardboard 18in. × 14in. 1974

Green and amber and gold it grows
  When the sun sinks late in the West;
And the breeze sweeps over the rippling rows
  Where the quail and the skylark nest.
Mountain or river or shining star,
  There's never a sight can beat—
Away to the sky-line stretching far—
  A sea of the ripening Wheat.

When the burning harvest sun sinks low,
  And shadows stretch on the plain,
The roaring strippers come and go
  Like ships on a sea of grain.
Till the lurching, groaning waggons bear
  Their tale of the load complete.
Of the world's great work he has done his share
  Who has garnered a crop of wheat.

Princes, Potentates, Kings and Czars,
  They travel in regal state,
But old King Wheat has a thousand cars
  For his trip to the water-gate;
And his thousand steamships breast the tide
  And plough through the wind and sleet
To the lands where the teeming millions bide
  That say: "Thank God for Wheat!"

Mulga Bill's Bicycle

'TWAS Mulga Bill, from Eaglehawk, that caught the cycling craze;
He turned away the good old horse that served him many days;
He dressed himself in cycling clothes, resplendent to be seen;
He hurried off to town and bought a shining new machine;
And as he wheeled it through the door, with air of lordly pride,
The grinning shop assistant said, "Excuse me, can you ride?"

"See here, young man," said Mulga Bill, "from Walgett to the sea,
From Conroy's Gap to Castlereagh, there's none can ride like me.
I'm good all round at everything, as everybody knows,
Although I'm not the one to talk—I hate a man that blows.

"But riding is my special gift, my chiefest, sole delight;
Just ask a wild duck can it swim, a wild cat can it fight.
There's nothing clothed in hair or hide, or built of flesh or steel,
There's nothing walks or jumps, or runs, on axle, hoof, or wheel,
But what I'll sit, while hide will hold and girths and straps are tight;
I'll ride this here two-wheeled concern right straight away at sight."

'Twas Mulga Bill, from Eaglehawk, that sought his own abode,
That perched above the Dead Man's Creek, beside the mountain
    road.
He turned the cycle down the hill and mounted for the fray,
But ere he'd gone a dozen yards it bolted clean away.
It left the track, and through the trees, just like a silver streak,
It whistled down the awful slope towards the Dead Man's Creek.

It shaved a stump by half an inch, it dodged a big white-box:
The very wallaroos in fright went scrambling up the rocks,
The wombats hiding in their caves dug deeper underground,
But Mulga Bill, as white às chalk, sat tight to every bound.
It struck a stone and gave a spring that cleared a fallen tree,
It raced beside a precipice as close as close could be;
And then, as Mulga Bill let out one last despairing shriek,
It made a leap of twenty feet into the Dead Man's Creek.

'Twas Mulga Bill, from Eaglehawk, that slowly swam ashore:
He said, "I've had some narrer shaves and lively rides before;
I've rode a wild bull round a yard to win a five-pound bet,
But this was sure the derndest ride that I've encountered yet.
I'll give that two-wheeled outlaw best; it's shaken all my nerve
To feel it whistle through the air and plunge and buck, and swerve,
It's safe at rest in Dead Man's Creek—we'll leave it lying still;
A horse's back is good enough henceforth for Mulga Bill."

MULGA BILL'S BICYCLE
Oil on canvas board 18in. × 14in. 1974

Waltzing Matilda

(Carrying a Swag)

OH! there once was a swagman camped in a Billabong,
  Under the shade of a Coolabah tree;
And he sang as he looked at his old billy boiling,
  "Who'll come a-waltzing Matilda with me?"

    Who'll come a-waltzing Matilda, my darling,
    Who'll come a-waltzing Matilda with me?
    Waltzing Matilda and leading a water-bag—
    Who'll come a-waltzing Matilda with me?

Down came a jumbuck to drink at the water-hole,
  Up jumped the swagman and grabbed him in glee;
And he sang as he stowed him away in his tucker-bag,
  "You'll come a-waltzing Matilda with me."

Down came the Squatter a-riding his thoroughbred;
  Down came Policemen—one, two and three.
    "Whose is the jumbuck you've got in the tucker-bag?
  You'll come a-waltzing Matilda with me."

But the swagman, he up and he jumped in the water-hole,
  Drowning himself by the Coolabah tree;
And his ghost may be heard as it sings in the Billabong
  "Who'll come a-waltzing Matilda with me?"

WALTZING MATILDA
Oil on hardboard 18in. × 14in. 1974

Saltbush Bill

Now this is the law of the Overland that all in the West obey—
A man must cover with travelling sheep a six-mile stage a day;
But this is the law which the drovers make, right easily understood,
They travel their stage where the grass is bad, but they camp
    where the grass is good;
They camp, and they ravage the squatter's grass till never a
    blade remains.
Then they drift away as the white clouds drift on the edge of the
    saltbush plains:
From camp to camp and from run to run they battle it hand to
    hand
For a blade of grass and the right to pass on the track of the
    Overland.
For this is the law of the Great Stock Routes, 'tis written in
    white and black—
The man that goes with a travelling mob must keep to a half-mile
    track;
And the drovers keep to a half-mile track on the runs where the
    grass is dead,
But they spread their sheep on a well-grassed run till they go
    with a two-mile spread.
So the squatters hurry the drovers on from dawn till the fall of
    night,
And the squatters' dogs and the drovers' dogs get mixed in a
    deadly fight.
Yet the squatters' men, though they haunt the mob, are willing
    the peace to keep,
For the drovers learn how to use their hands when they go with
    the travelling sheep;
But this is the tale of a Jackeroo that came from a foreign strand,
And the fight that he fought with Saltbush Bill, the King of
    the Overland.

Now Saltbush Bill was a drover tough as ever the country knew,
He had fought his way on the Great Stock Routes from the sea
    to the big Barcoo;
He could tell when he came to a friendly run that gave him a
    chance to spread,
And he knew where the hungry owners were that hurried his
    sheep ahead;
He was drifting down in the Eighty drought with a mob that
    could scarcely creep
(When the kangaroos by the thousand starve, it is rough on the
    travelling sheep),

SALTBUSH BILL
Oil on canvas board 18in. × 14in. 1974

And he camped one night at the crossing-place on the edge of
the Wilga run;
"We must manage a feed for them here," he said, "or half of the
mob are done!"
So he spread them out when they left the camp wherever they
liked to go,
Till he grew aware of a Jackeroo with a station-hand in tow.
They set to work on the straggling sheep, and with many a stock-
whip crack
They forced them in where the grass was dead in the space of
the half-mile track;
And William prayed that the hand of Fate might suddenly strike
him blue
But he'd get some grass for his starving sheep in the teeth of that
Jackeroo.
So he turned and he cursed the Jackeroo; he cursed him, alive
or dead,
From the soles of his great unwieldly feet to the crown of his
ugly head,
With an extra curse on the moke he rode and the cur at his heels
that ran,
Till the Jackaroo from his horse got down and went for the drover-
man;
With the station-hand for his picker-up, though the sheep ran
loose the while,
They battled it out on the well-grassed plain in the regular prize-
ring style.

Now, the new chum fought for his honour's sake and the pride
of the English race,
But the drover fought for his daily bread with a smile on his
bearded face;
So he shifted ground, and he sparred for wind, and he made it
a lengthy mill,
And from time to time as his scouts came in they whispered to
Saltbush Bill—
"We have spread the sheep with a two-mile spread, and the grass
it is something grand;
You must stick to him, Bill, for another round for the pride of
the Overland."

The new chum made it a rushing fight, though never a blow
   got home,
Till the sun rode high in the cloudless sky and glared on the
   brick-red loam,
Till the sheep drew in to the shelter-trees and settled them down
   to rest;
Then the drover said he would fight no more, and gave his
   opponent best.

So the new chum rode to the homestead straight, and told them a
   story grand
Of the desperate fight that he fought that day with the King
   of the Overland;
And the tale went home to the Public Schools of the pluck of the
   English swell—
How the drover fought for his very life, but blood in the end
   must tell.
But the travelling sheep and the Wilga sheep were boxed on the
   Old Man Plain;
'Twas a full week's work ere they drafted out and hunted them
   off again;
A week's good grass in their wretched hides, with a curse and a
   stockwhip crack
They hunted them off on the road once more to starve on the
   half-mile track.
And Saltbush Bill, on the Overland, will many a time recite
How the best day's work that he ever did was the day that he
   lost the fight.

In Defence of the Bush

So you're back from up the country, Mister Lawson, where you
    went,
And you're cursing all the business in a bitter discontent;
Well, we grieve to disappoint you, and it makes us sad to hear
That it wasn't cool and shady—and there wasn't whips of beer,
And the looney bullock snorted when you first came into view—
Well, you know it's not so often that he sees a swell like you;
And the roads were hot and dusty, and the plains were burnt
    and brown,
And no doubt you're better suited drinking lemon-squash in town.
Yet, perchance, if you should journey down the very track you
    went
In a month or two at furthest, you would wonder what it meant;
Where the sunbaked earth was gasping like a creature in its pain
You would find the grasses waving like a field of summer grain,
And the miles of thirsty gutters, blocked with sand and choked
    with mud,
You would find them mighty rivers with a turbid, sweeping flood.
For the rain and drought and sunshine make no changes in the
    street,
In the sullen line of buildings and the ceaseless tramp of feet;
But the bush has moods and changes, as the seasons rise and fall,
And the men who know the bush-land—they are loyal through it all.

    .   .   .   .   .   .

But you found the bush was dismal and a land of no delight—
Did you chance to hear a chorus in the shearers' huts at night?
Did they "rise up William Riley" by the camp-fire's cheery blaze?
Did they rise him as we rose him in the good old droving days?
And the women of the homesteads and the men you chanced to
    meet—
Were their faces sour and saddened like the "faces in the street"?
And the "shy selector children"—were they better now or worse
Than the little city urchins who would greet you with a curse?
Is not such a life much better than the squalid street and square
Where the fallen women flaunt it in the fierce electric glare,
Where the sempstress plies her needle till her eyes are sore and red
In a filthy, dirty attic toiling on for daily bread?

IN DEFENCE OF THE BUSH
Oil on canvas board 18in. × 14in. 1974

Did you hear no sweeter voices in the music of the bush
Than the roar of trams and buses, and the war-whoop of "the push"?
Did the magpies rouse your slumbers with their carol sweet and
    strange?
Did you hear the silver chiming of the bell-birds on the range?
But, perchance, the wild birds' music by your senses was despised,
For you say you'll stay in townships till the bush is civilized.
Would you make it a tea-garden, and on Sundays have a band
Where the "blokes" might take their "donahs", with a "public"
    close at hand?
You had better stick to Sydney and make merry with the "push",
For the bush will never suit you, and you'll never suit the bush.

When Dacey Rode the Mule

'TWAS to a small, up-country town,
  When we were boys at school,
There came a circus with a clown,
  Likewise a bucking mule.
The clown announced a scheme they had
  Spectators for to bring—
They'd give a crown to any lad
  Who'd ride him round the ring.

And, gentle reader, do not scoff
  Nor think a man a fool—
To buck a porous-plaster off
  Was pastime to that mule.

The boys got on he bucked like sin;
  He threw them in the dirt.
What time the clown would raise a grin
  By asking, "Are you hurt?"
But Johnny Dacey came one night,
  The crack of all the school;
Said he, "I'll win the crown all right;
  Bring in your bucking mule."

The elephant went off his trunk,
  The monkey played the fool,
And all the band got blazing drunk
  When Dacey rode the mule.

But soon there rose a galling shout
  Of laughter, for the clown
From somewhere in his pants drew out
  A little paper crown.
He placed the crown on Dacey's head
  While Dacey looked a fool;
"Now, there's your crown, my lad," he said,
  "For riding of the mule!"

The band struck up with "Killaloe",
  And "Rule Britannia, Rule",
And "Young Man from the Country", too,
  When Dacey rode the mule.
Then Dacey, in a furious rage,
  For vengeance on the show
Ascended to the monkeys' cage
  And let the monkeys go;
The blue-tailed ape and the chimpanzee
  He turned abroad to roam;
Good faith! It was a sight to see
  The people step for home.

For big baboons with canine snout
   Are spiteful, as a rule—
The people didn't sit it out,
   When Dacey rode the mule.

And from the beasts he let escape,
   The bushmen all declare,
Were·born some creatures partly ape
   And partly native-bear.
They're rather few and far between,
   The race is nearly spent;
But some of them may still be seen
   In Sydney Parliament.

And when those legislators fight,
   And drink, and act the fool,
Just blame it on that torrid night
   When Dacey rode the mule.

WHEN DACEY RODE THE MULE
Oil on canvas board 18in. × 14in. 1974

Shearing at Castlereagh

THE bell is set a-ringing, and the engine gives a toot,
There's five-and-thirty shearers here a-shearing for the loot,
So stir yourselves, you penners-up, and shove the sheep along—
The musterers are fetching them a hundred thousand strong—
And make your collie dogs speak up; what would the buyers say
In London if the wool was late this year from Castlereagh?

The man that "rung" the Tubbo shed is not the ringer here,
That stripling from the Cooma-side can teach him how to shear.
They trim away the ragged locks, and rip the cutter goes,
And leaves a track of snowy fleece from brisket to the nose;
It's lovely how they peel it off with never stop nor stay,
They're racing for the ringer's place this year at Castlereagh.

The man that keeps the cutters sharp is growling in his cage,
He's always in a hurry; and he's always in a rage—
"You clumsy-fisted mutton-heads, you'd turn a fellow sick,
You pass yourselves as shearers, you were born to swing a pick.
Another broken cutter here, that's two you've broke today,
It's lovely how they peel it off with never stop nor stay,

The youngsters picking up the fleece enjoy the merry din,
They throw the classer up the fleece, he throws it to the bin;
The pressers standing by the rack are waiting for the wool,
There's room for just a couple more, the press is nearly full;
Now jump upon the lever, lads, and heave and heave away,
Another bale of golden fleece is branded "Castlereagh".

SHEARING AT CASTLEREAGH
Oil on canvas board 18in. × 14in. 1974

The First Surveyor

"THE opening of the railway line!—the Governor and all!
With flags and banners down the street, a banquet and a ball.
Hark to 'em at the station now! They're raising cheer on cheer!
'The man who brought the railway through—our friend the
      engineer.'

"They cheer *his* pluck and enterprise and engineering skill!
'Twas my old husband found the pass behind that big red hill.
Before the engineer was born we'd settled with our stock
Behind that great big mountain chain, a line of range and rock—
A line that kept us starving there in weary weeks of drought,
With ne'er a track across the range to let the cattle out.

" 'Twas then, with horses starved and weak and scarcely fit to crawl,
My husband went to find a way across the rocky wall.
He vanished in the wilderness—God knows where he was gone—
He hunted till his food gave out, but still he battled on.
His horses strayed ('twas well they did), they made towards the
      grass,
And down behind that big red hill they found an easy pass.

"He followed up and blazed the trees, to show the safest track,
Then drew his belt another hole and turned and started back.
His horses died—just one pulled through with nothing much to
      spare;
God bless the beast that brought him home, the old white Arab
      mare!
We drove the cattle through the hills, along the new-found way,
And this was our first camping-ground—just where I live today.

"Then others came across the range and built the township here,
And then there came the railway line and this young engineer;
He drove about with tents and traps, a cook to cook his meals,
A bath to wash himself at night, a chain-man at his heels.
And that was all the pluck and skill for which he's cheered and
      praised,
For after all he took the track, the same my husband blazed!

"My poor old husband, dead and gone with never feast nor cheer;
He's buried by the railway line!—I wonder can he hear
When by the very track he marked, and close to where he's laid,
The cattle trains go roaring down the one-in-thirty grade.
I wonder does he hear them pass, and can he see the sight
When, whistling shrill, the fast express goes flaming by at night.

THE FIRST SURVEYOR
Oil on canvas board 18in. × 14in. 1974

"I think 'twould comfort him to know there's someone left to care;
I'll take some things this very night and hold a banquet there—
The hard old fare we've often shared together, him and me,
Some damper and a bite of beef, a pannikin of tea:
We'll do without the bands and flags, the speeches and the fuss,
We know who *ought* to get the cheers—and that's enough for us.

"What's that? They wish that I'd come down—the oldest settler
    here!
Present me to the Governor and that young engineer!
Well, just you tell his Excellence, and put the thing polite,
I'm sorry, but I can't come down—I'm dining out tonight!"

How Gilbert Died

THERE'S never a stone at the sleeper's head,
  There's never a fence beside,
And the wandering stock on the grave may tread
  Unnoticed and undenied;
But the smallest child on the Watershed
  Can tell you how Gilbert died.

For he rode at dusk with his comrade Dunn
  To the hut at the Stockman's Ford;
In the waning light of the sinking sun
  They peered with a fierce accord.
They were outlaws both—and on each man's head
  Was a thousand pounds reward.

They had taken toll of the country round,
  And the troopers came behind
With a black who tracked like a human hound
  In the scrub and the ranges blind:
He could run the trail where a white man's eye
  No sign of track could find.

He had hunted them out of the One Tree Hill
  And over the Old Man Plain,
But they wheeled their tracks with a wild beast's skill,
  And they made for the range again;
Then away to the hut where their grandsire dwelt
  They rode with a loosened rein.

And their grandsire gave them a greeting bold:
  "Come in and rest in peace,
No safer place does the country hold—
  With the night pursuit must cease,
And we'll drink success to the roving boys,
  And to hell with the black police."

But they went to death when they entered there
  In the hut at the Stockman's Ford,
For their grandsire's words were as false as fair—
  They were doomed to the hangman's cord.
He had sold them both to the black police
  For the sake of the big reward.

In the depth of night there are forms that glide
  As stealthily as serpents creep,
And around the hut where the outlaws hide
  They plant in the shadows deep,
And they wait till the first faint flush of dawn
  Shall waken their prey from sleep.

But Gilbert wakes while the night is dark—
    A restless sleeper aye.
He has heard the sound of a sheep-dog's bark,
    And his horse's warning neigh,
And he says to his mate, "There are hawks abroad,
    And it's time that we went away."

Their rifles stood at the stretcher head,
    Their bridles lay to hand;
They wakened the old man out of his bed,
    When they heard the sharp command:
"In the name of the Queen lay down your arms,
    Now, Dunn and Gilbert, stand!"

Then Gilbert reached for his rifle true
    That close at hand he kept;
He pointed straight at the voice, and drew,
    But never a flash outleapt,
For the water ran from the rifle breech—
    It was drenched while the outlaws slept.

Then he dropped the piece with a bitter oath,
    And he turned to his comrade Dunn:
"We are sold," he said, "we are dead men both!—
    Still, there may be a chance for one;
I'll stop and I'll fight with the pistol here,
    You take to your heels and run."

So Dunn crept out on his hands and knees
    In the dim, half-dawning light,
And he made his way to a patch of trees,
    And was lost in the black of night;
And the trackers hunted his tracks all day,
    But they never could trace his flight.

But Gilbert walked from the open door
    In a confident style and rash;
He heard at his side the rifles roar,
    And he heard the bullets crash.
But he laughed as he lifted his pistol-hand,
    And he fired at the rifle flash.

Then out of the shadows the troopers aimed
    At his voice and the pistol sound.
With rifle flashes the darkness flamed—
    He staggered and spun around,
And they riddled his body with rifle balls
    As it lay on the blood-soaked ground.

HOW GILBERT DIED
Oil on canvas board 18in. × 14in. 1974

There's never a stone at the sleeper's head,
  There's never a fence beside,
And the wandering stock on the grave may tread
  Unnoticed and undenied;
But the smallest child on the Watershed
  Can tell you how Gilbert died.

The Man From Ironbark

It was the man from Ironbark who struck the Sydney town,
He wandered over street and park, he wandered up and down.
He loitered here, he loitered there, till he was like to drop,
Until at last in sheer despair he sought a barber's shop.
" 'Ere! shave my beard and whiskers off, I'll be a man of mark,
I'll go and do the Sydney toff up home in Ironbark."

The barber man was small and flash, as barbers mostly are,
He wore a strike-your-fancy sash, he smoked a huge cigar:
He was a humorist of note and keen at repartee,
He laid the odds and kept a "tote", whatever that may be.
And when he saw our friend arrive, he whispered "Here's a lark!
Just watch me catch him all alive this man from Ironbark."

There were some gilded youths that sat along the barber's wall,
Their eyes were dull, their heads were flat, they had no brains
        at all;
To them the barber passed the wink, his dexter eyelid shut,
"I'll make this bloomin' yokel think his bloomin' throat is cut."
And as he soaped and rubbed it in he made a rude remark:
"I s'pose the flats is pretty green up there in Ironbark."

A grunt was all reply he got; he shaved the bushman's chin,
Then made the water boiling hot and dipped the razor in.
He raised his hand, his brow grew black, he paused awhile to
        gloat,
Then slashed the red-hot razor-back across his victim's throat;
Upon the newly-shaven skin it made a livid mark—
No doubt it fairly took him in—the man from Ironbark.

He fetched a wild up-country yell might wake the dead to hear,
And though his throat, he knew full well, was cut from ear to ear,
He struggled gamely to his feet, and faced the murderous foe.
"You've done for me! you dog, I'm beat! one hit before I go!
I only wish I had a knife, you blessed murdering shark!
But you'll remember all your life the man from Ironbark."

He lifted up his hairy paw, with one tremendous clout
He landed on the barber's jaw, and knocked the barber out.
He set to work with tooth and nail, he made the place a wreck;
He grabbed the nearest gilded youth, and tried to break his neck.
And all the while his throat he held to save his vital spark,
And "Murder! Bloody Murder!" yelled the man from Ironbark.

A peeler man who heard the din came in to see the show;
He tried to run the bushman in, but he refused to go.
And when at last the barber spoke, and said " 'Twas all in fun—
'Twas just a little harmless joke, a trifle overdone."
"A joke!" he cried, "By George, that's fine; a lively sort of lark;
I'd like to catch that murdering swine some night in Ironbark."

And now while round the shearing-floor the listening shearers gape,
He tells the story o'er and o'er and brags of his escape.
"Them barber chaps what keeps a tote, by George, I've had enough,
One tried to cut my bloomin' throat, but thank the Lord it's tough."
And whether he's believed or no, there's one thing to remark,
That flowing beards are all the go way up in Ironbark.

THE MAN FROM IRONBARK
Oil on hardboard 18in. × 14in. 1974

A Bush Christening

On the outer Barcoo where the churches are few,
   And men of religion are scanty,
On a road never cross'd 'cept by folk that are lost
   One Michael Magee had a shanty.

Now this Mike was the dad of a ten-year-old lad,
   Plump, healthy, and stoutly conditioned;
He was strong as the best, but poor Mike had no rest
   For the youngster had never been christened.

And his wife used to cry, "If the darlin' should die
   Saint Peter would not recognize him."
But by luck he survived till a preacher arrived,
   Who agreed straightaway to baptize him.

Now the artful young rogue, while they held their collogue,
   With his ear to the keyhole was listenin';
And he muttered in fright, while his features turned white,
   "What the devil and all is this christenin'?"

He was none of your dolts—he had seen them brand colts.
   And it seemed to his small understanding,
If the man in the frock made him one of the flock,
   It must mean something very like branding.

So away with a rush he set off for the bush,
   While the tears in his eyelids they glistened—
" 'Tis outrageous," says he, "to brand youngsters like me;
   I'll be dashed if I'll stop to be christened!"

Like a young native dog he ran into a log,
   And his father with language uncivil,
Never heeding the "praste", cried aloud in his haste
   "Come out and be christened, you divil!"

But he lay there as snug as a bug in a rug,
   And his parents in vain might reprove him,
Till his reverence spoke (he was fond of a joke)
   "I've a notion," says he, "that'll move him.

"Poke a stick up the log, give the spalpeen a prog;
   Poke him aisy—don't hurt him or maim him;
'Tis not long that he'll stand, I've the water at hand,
   As he rushes out this end I'll name him.

"Here he comes, and for shame! ye've forgotten the name—
   Is it Patsy or Michael or Dinnis?"
Here the youngster ran out, and the priest gave a shout—
   "Take your chance, anyhow, wid 'Maginnis!' "

A BUSH CHRISTENING
Oil on harboard 18in. × 24in. 1974

As the howling young cub ran away to the scrub
   Where he knew that pursuit would be risky,
The priest, as he fled, flung a flask at his head
   That was labelled "Maginnis's Whisky"!

Now Maginnis Magee has been made a J.P.,
   And the one thing he hates more than sin is
To be asked by the folk, who have heard of the joke,
   How he came to be christened Maginnis!

In the Droving Days

"ONLY a pound," said the auctioneer,
"Only a pound; and I'm standing here
Selling this animal, gain or loss—
Only a pound for the drover's horse?
One of the sort that was ne'er afraid,
One of the boys of the Old Brigade;
Thoroughly honest and game, I'll swear,
Only a little the worse for wear;
Plenty as bad to be seen in town,
Give me a bid and I'll knock him down;
Sold as he stands, and without recourse,
Give me a bid for the drover's horse."

Loitering there in an aimless way
Somehow I noticed the poor old grey,
Weary and battered and screwed, of course;
Yet when I noticed the old grey horse,
The rough bush saddle, and single rein
Of the bridle laid on his tangled mane,
Straightway the crowd and the auctioneer
Seemed on a sudden to disappear,
Melted away in a kind of haze—
For my heart went back to the droving days.

Back to the road, and I crossed again
Over the miles of the saltbush plain—
The shining plain that is said to be
The dried-up bed of an inland sea.
Where the air so dry and so clear and bright
Refracts the sun with a wondrous light,
And out in the dim horizon makes
The deep blue gleam of the phantom lakes.

At dawn of day we could feel the breeze
That stirred the boughs of the sleeping trees,
And brought a breath of the fragrance rare
That comes and goes in that scented air;
For the trees and grass and the shrubs contain
A dry sweet scent on the saltbush plain.
For those that love it and understand
The saltbush plain is a wonderland,
A wondrous country, where Nature's ways
Were revealed to me in the droving days.

We saw the fleet wild horses pass,
And kangaroos through the Mitchell grass;
The emu ran with her frightened brood
All unmolested and unpursued.
But there rose a shout and a wild hubbub
When the dingo raced for his native scrub,
And he paid right dear for his stolen meals
With the drovers' dogs at his wretched heels.
For we ran him down at a rattling pace,
While the pack-horse joined in the stirring chase.
And a wild halloo at the kill we'd raise—
We were light of heart in the droving days.

'Twas a drover's horse, and my hand again
Made a move to close on a fancied rein.
For I felt the swing and the easy stride
Of the grand old horse that I used to ride.
In drought or plenty, in good or ill,
The same old steed was my comrade still;
The old grey horse with his honest ways
Was a mate to me in the droving days.

When we kept our watch in the cold and damp,
If the cattle broke from the sleeping camp,
Over the flats and across the plain,
With my head bent down on his waving mane,
Through the boughs above and the stumps below,
On the darkest night I could let him go
At a racing speed; he would choose his course,
And my life was safe with the old grey horse.
But man and horse had a favourite job,
When an outlaw broke from a station mob;
With a right good will was the stockwhip plied,
As the old horse raced at the straggler's side,
And the greenhide whip such a weal would raise—
We could use the whip in the droving days.

. . . . .

"Only a pound!" and was this the end—
Only a pound for the drover's friend.
The drover's friend that has seen his day,
And now was worthless and cast away
With a broken knee and a broken heart
To be flogged and starved in a hawker's cart.
Well, I made a bid for a sense of shame.
And the memories dear of the good old game.

IN THE DROVING DAYS
Oil on canvas board 18in. × 14in. 1974

"Thank you? Guinea! and cheap at that!
Against you there in the curly hat!
Only a guinea, and one more chance,
Down he goes if there's no advance,
Third, and last time, one! two! three!"
And the old grey horse was knocked down to me.
And now he's wandering, fat and sleek,
On the lucerne flats by the Homestead Creek;
I dare not ride him for fear he'd fall,
But he does a journey to beat them all,
For though he scarcely a trot can raise,
He can take me back to the droving days.

Song of the Artesian Water

Now the stock have started dying, for the Lord has sent a drought;
But we're sick of prayers and Providence—we're going to do without;
With the derricks up above us and the solid earth below,
We are waiting at the lever for the word to let her go.
    Sinking down, deeper down
     Oh, we'll sink it deeper down:
As the drill is plugging downward at a thousand feet of level,
If the Lord won't send us water, oh, we'll get it from the devil;
Yes, we'll get it from the devil deeper down.

Now, our engine's built in Glasgow by a very canny Scot,
And he marked it twenty horse-power, but he don't know what is
   what:
When Canadian Bill is firing with the sun-dried gidgee logs,
She can equal thirty horses and a score or so of dogs.
    Sinking down, deeper down,
     Oh, we're going deeper down:
If we fail to get the water, then it's ruin to the squatter,
For the drought is on the station and the weather's growing hotter,
But we're bound to get the water deeper down.

But the shaft has started caving and the sinking's very slow,
And the yellow rods are bending in the water down below,
And the tubes are always jamming and they can't be made to shift
Till we nearly burst the engine with a forty horse-power lift.
    Sinking down, deeper down,
     Oh, we're going deeper down:
Though the shaft is always caving, and the tubes are always jamming,
Yet we'll fight our way to water while the stubborn drill is ramming—
While the stubborn drill is ramming deeper down.

But there's no artesian water, though we've passed three thousand
  feet,
And the contract price is growing, and the boss is nearly beat.
But it must be down beneath us, and it's down we've got to go,
Though she's bumping on the solid rock four thousand feet below.
    Sinking down, deeper down,
     Oh, we're going deeper down:
And it's time they heard us knocking on the roof of Satan's dwellin';
But we'll get artesian water if we cave the roof of hell in—
Oh! we'll get artesian water deeper down.

But it's hark! the whistle's blowing with a wild, exultant blast,
And the boys are madly cheering, for they've struck the flow at
        last;
And it's rushing up the tubing from four thousand feet below,
Till it spouts above the casing in a million-gallon flow.
        And it's down, deeper down—
        Oh, it comes from deeper down;
It is flowing, ever flowing, in a free, unstinted measure
From the silent hidden places where the old earth hides her treasure—
Where the old earth hides her treasures deeper down.

And it's clear away the timber, and it's let the water run;
How it glimmers in the shadow, how it flashes in the sun!
By the silent belts of timber, by the miles of blazing plain
It is bringing hope and comfort to the thirsty land again.
        Flowing down, further down;
        It is flowing further down
To the tortured thirsty cattle, bringing gladness in its going;
Through the droughty days of summer it is flowing, ever flowing—
It is flowing, ever flowing, further down.

SONG OF THE ARTESIAN WATER
Oil on canvas board 18in. × 14in. 1974

Johnson's Antidote

DOWN along the Snakebite River where the overlanders camp,
Where the serpents are in millions, all of the most deadly stamp;
Where the station-cook in terror, nearly every time he bakes,
Mixes up among the doughboys half a dozen poison-snakes;
Where the wily free-selector walks in armour-plated pants,
And defies the stings of scorpions, and the bites of bull-dog ants:
Where the adder and the viper tear each other by the throat—
There it was that William Johnson sought his snake-bite antidote.

Johnson was a free-selector, and his brain went rather queer,
For the constant sight of serpents filled him with a deadly fear;
So he tramped his free-selection, morning, afternoon, and night,
Seeking for some great specific that would cure the serpent's bite
Till King Billy, of the Mooki, chieftain of the flour-bag head,
Told him, "Spos'n snake bite pfeller, pfellar mostly drop down dead;
Spos'n snake bite old goanna, then you watch a while you see
Old goanna cure himself with eating little pfeller tree."
"That's the cure," said William Johnson, "point me out this plant
    sublime."
But King Billy, feeling lazy, said he'd go another time.
Thus it came to pass that Johnson, having got the tale by rote,
Followed every stray goanna seeking for the antidote.

            .   .   .   .

Loafing once beside the river, while he thought his heart would
    break,
There he saw a big goanna fight with a tiger-snake.
In and out they rolled and wriggled, bit each other, heart and soul,
Till the valiant old goanna swallowed his opponent whole.
Breathless, Johnson sat and watched him, saw him struggle up the
    bank,
Saw him nibbling at the branches of some bushes, green and rank;
Saw him, happy and contented, lick his lips, as off he crept,
While the bulging of his stomach showed where his opponent slept
Then a cheer of exultation burst aloud from Johnson's throat;
"Luck at last," said he, "I've struck it! 'tis the famous antidote.

JOHNSON'S ANTIDOTE
Oil on canvas board 18in. × 14in. 1974

"Here it is, the Grand Elixir, greatest blessing ever known—
Twenty thousand men in India die each year of snakes alone;
Think of all the foreign nations, negro, chow, and blackamoor,
Saved from sudden expiration by my wondrous snakebite cure.
It will bring me fame and fortune! In the happy days to be
Men of every clime and nation will be round to gaze on me—
Scientific men in thousands, men of mark and men of note,
Rushing down the Mooki River, after Johnson's antidote.
It will cure *delirium tremens* when the patient's eyeballs stare
At imaginary spiders, snakes which really are not there.
When he thinks he sees them wriggle, when he thinks he sees them
      bloat,
It will cure him just to think of Johnson's Snakebite Antidote."

Then he rushed to the museum, found a scientific man—
"Trot me out a deadly serpent, just the deadliest you can;
I intend to let him bite me, all the risk I will endure.
Just to prove the sterling value of my wondrous snakebite cure.
Even though an adder bit me, back to life again I'd float;
Snakes are out of date, I tell you, since I've found the antidote."
Said the scientific person, "If you really want to die,
Go ahead—but, if you're doubtful, let your sheep-dog have a try.
Get a pair of dogs and try it, let the snake give both a nip;
Give your dog the snakebite mixture, let the other fellow rip;
If he dies and yours survives him then it proves the thing is good.
Will you fetch your dog and try it?" Johnson rather thought he
      would.
So he went and fetched his canine, hauled him forward by the throat.
"Stump, old man," says he, "we'll show them we've the genwine
      antidote."

JOHNSON'S ANTIDOTE
Oil on canvas board 16in. × 14in. 1974

Both the dogs were duly loaded with the poison-gland's contents;
Johnson gave his dog the mixture, then sat down to wait events.
"Mark," he said, "in twenty minutes Stump'll be a-rushing round,
While the other wretched creature lies a corpse upon the ground."
But, alas for William Johnson! ere they'd watched a half-hour's spell
Stumpy was as dead as mutton, t'other dog was live and well.
And the scientific person hurried off with utmost speed,
Tested Johnson's drug and found it was a deadly poison-weed;
Half a tumbler killed an emu, half a spoonful killed a goat—
All the snakes on earth were harmless to that awful antidote.
Down along the Mooki River, on the overlanders' camp,
Where the serpents are in millions, all of the most deadly stamp,
Wanders, daily, William Johnson, down among those poisonous
    hordes,
Shooting every stray goanna calls them "black and yaller frauds".
And King Billy, of the Mooki, cadging for the cast-off coat,
Somehow seems to dodge the subject of the snakebite antidote.

Only a Jockey

"Richard Bennison, a jockey, aged fourteen, while riding William Tell in his training, was thrown and killed. The horse is luckily uninjured."—Melbourne Wire.

OUT in the grey cheerless chill of the morning light,
  Out on the track where the night shades still lurk,
Ere the first gleam of the sungod's returning light
  Round come the racehorses early at work.

Reefing and pulling and racing so readily,
  Close sit the jockey-boys holding them hard,
"Steady the stallion there—canter him steadily,
  Don't let him gallop so much as a yard."

Fiercely he fights while the others run wide of him,
  Reefs at the bit that would hold him in thrall,
Plunges and bucks till the boy that's astride of him
  Goes to the ground with a terrible fall.

"Stop him there! Block him there! Drive him in carefully,
  Lead him about till he's quiet and cool.
Sound as a bell! though he's blown himself fearfully,
  Now let us pick up this poor little fool.

"Stunned? Oh, by Jove, I'm afraid it's a case with him;
  Ride for the doctor! keep bathing his head!
Send for a cart to go down to our place with him"—
  No use! One long sigh and the little chap's dead.

Only a jockey-boy, foul-mouthed and bad you see,
  Ignorant, heathenish, gone to his rest.
Parson or Presbyter, Pharisee, Sadducee,
  What did you do for him?—bad was the best.

Negroes and foreigners, all have a claim on you;
  Yearly you send your well-advertised hoard,
But the poor jockey-boy—shame on you, shame on you,
  "Feed ye My little ones"—what said the Lord?

Him ye held less than the outer barbarian,
  Left him to die in his ignorant sin;
Have you no principles, humanitarian?
  Have you no precept—"Go gather them in?"

73

Knew he God's name? In his brutal profanity
That name was an oath—out of many but one.
What did he get from our famed Christianity?
Where has his soul—if he had any—gone?

Fourteen years old, and what was he taught of it?
What did he know of God's infinite Grace?
Draw the dark curtain of shame o'er the thought of it
Draw the shroud over the jockey-boy's face.

ONLY A JOCKEY
Oil on canvas board 18in. × 14in. 1974

Been There Before

THERE came a stranger to Walgett town,
  To Walgett town when the sun was low,
And he carried a thirst that was worth a crown,
  Yet how to quench it he did not know;
But he thought he might take those yokels down,
The guileless yokels of Walgett town.

They made him a bet in a private bar,
  In a private bar when the talk was high,
And they bet him some pounds no matter how far
  He could pelt a stone, yet he could not shy
A stone right over the river so brown,
The Darling River at Walgett town.

He knew that the river from bank to bank
  Was fifty yards, and he smiled a smile
As he trundled down; but his hopes they sank,
  For there wasn't a stone within fifty mile;
For the saltbush plain and the open down
Produce no quarries in Walgett town.

The yokels laughed at his hopes o'erthrown,
  And he stood awhile like a man in a dream;
Then he out of his pocket he fetched a stone,
  And pelted it over the silent stream—
He'd been there before; he had wandered down
On a previous visit to Walgett town.

BEEN THERE BEFORE
Oil on canvas board 18in. × 14in. 1974

City of Dreadful Thirst

THE stranger came from Narromine and made his little joke;
"They say we folks in Narromine are narrow-minded folk;
But all the smartest men down here are puzzled to define
A kind of new phenomenon that came to Narromine.

"Last summer up in Narromine 'twas gettin' rather warm—
Two hundred in the water-bag, and lookin' like a storm—
We all were in the private bar, the coolest place in town,
When out across the stretch of plain a cloud came rollin' down.

"We don't respect the clouds up there, they fill us with disgust,
They mostly bring a Bogan shower—three raindrops and some dust;
But each man, simultaneous-like, to each man said, 'I think
That cloud suggests it's up to us to have another drink!'

"There's clouds of rain and clouds of dust—we'd heard of them
    before,
And sometimes in the daily press we read of 'clouds of war'.
But—if this ain't the Gospel truth I hope that I may burst—
That cloud that came to Narromine was just a cloud of thirst.

"It wasn't like a common cloud, 'twas more a sort of haze;
It settled down about the street, and stopped for days and days;
And not a drop of dew could fall, and not a sunbeam shine
To pierce that dismal sort of mist that hung on Narromine.

"Oh, Lord! we had a dreadful time beneath that cloud of thirst!
We all chucked-up our daily work and went upon the burst.
The very blacks about the town, that used to cadge for grub,
They made an organized attack and tried to loot the pub.

"We couldn't leave the private bar no matter how we tried;
Shearers and squatters, union-men and blacklegs side by side
Were drinkin' there and dursn't move, for each was sure, he said,
Before he'd get a half-a-mile the thirst would strike him dead!

"We drank until the drink gave out; we searched from room to room,
And round the pub, like drunken ghosts, went howling through
    the gloom.
The shearers found some kerosene and settled down again,
But all the squatter chaps and I, we staggered to the train.

"And once outside the cloud of thirst we felt as right as pie,
But while we stopped about the town we had to drink or die.
I hear today it's safe enough; I'm going back to work
Because they say the cloud of thirst has shifted on to Bourke.

CITY OF DREADFUL THIRST
Oil on hardboard 18in. × 14in. 1974

"But when you see those clouds about—like this one over here—
All white and frothy at the top, just like a pint of beer,
It's time to go and have a drink, for if that cloud should burst
You'd find the drink would all be gone, for that's a cloud of thirst!"

                    .   .   .   .   .   .

We stood the man from Narromine a pint of half-and-half;
He drank it off without a gasp in one tremendous quaff;
"I joined some friends last night," he said, "in what *they* called a
        spree;
But after Narromine 'twas just a holiday to me.

And now beyond the Western Range, where sunset skies are red,
And clouds of dust, and clouds of thirst, go drifting overhead,
The railway-train is taking back, along the Western Line,
That narrow-minded person on his road to Narromine.

THE TRAVELLING POST OFFICE
Oil on hardboard 35 x 45 cm 1976

Old Pardon, the Son of Reprieve

You never heard tell of the story?
   Well, now, I can hardly believe!
Never heard of the honour and glory
   Of Pardon, the son of Reprieve?
But maybe you're only a Johnnie
   And don't know a horse from a hoe?
Well, well, don't get angry, my sonny,
   But, really, a young un should know.

They bred him out back on the "Never",
   His mother was Mameluke breed.
To the front — and then stay there — was ever
   The root of the Mameluke creed.
He seemed to inherit their wiry
   Strong frames — and their pluck to receive —
As hard as a flint and as fiery
   Was Pardon, the son of Reprieve.

We ran him at many a meeting
   At crossing and gully and town,
And nothing could give him a beating —
   At least when our money was down.
For weight wouldn't stop him, nor distance,
   Nor odds, though the others were fast;
He'd race with a dogged persistence,
   And wear them all down at the last.

At the Turon the Yattendon filly
   Led by lengths at the mile-and-a-half,
And we all began to look silly,
   While her crowd were starting to laugh;
But the old horse came faster and faster,
   His pluck told its tale, and his strength,
He gained on her, caught her, and passed her,
   And won it, hands-down, by a length.

And then we swooped down on Menindie
   To run for the President's Cup;
Oh! that's a sweet township — a shindy
   To them is board, lodging, and sup.
Eye-openers they are, and their system
   Is never to suffer defeat;
It's "win, tie, or wrangle" — to best 'em
   You must lose 'em, or else it's "dead heat".

OLD PARDON, THE SON OF REPRIEVE I
Oil on hardboard 46 x 68 cm 1976

We strolled down the township and found 'em
  At drinking and gaming and play;
If sorrows they had, why they drowned 'em,
  And betting was soon under way.
Their horses were good uns and fit uns,
  There was plenty of cash in the town;
They backed their own horses like Britons,
  And, Lord! how *we* rattled it down!

With gladness we thought of the morrow,
  We counted our wages with glee,
A simile homely to borrow —
  "There was plenty of milk in our tea."
You see we were green; and we never
  Had even a thought of foul play,
Though we well might have known that the clever
  Division would "put us away".

Experience *docet*, they tell us,
  At least so I've frequently heard;
But, "dosing" or "stuffing", those fellows
  Were up to each move on the board:
They got to his stall — it is sinful
  To think what such villains will do —
And they gave him a regular skinful
  Of barley — green barley — to chew.

He munched it all night, and we found him
  Next morning as full as a hog —
The girths wouldn't nearly meet round him;
  He looked like an overfed frog.
We saw we were done like a dinner —
  The odds were a thousand to one
Against Pardon turning up winner,
  'Twas cruel to ask him to run.

We got to the course with our troubles,
  A crestfallen couple were we;
And we heard the "books" calling the doubles —
  A roar like the surf of the sea;
And over the tumult and louder
  Rang "Any price Pardon, I lay!"
Says Jimmy, "The children of Judah
  Are out on the warpath today."

OLD PARDON, THE SON OF REPRIEVE II
Oil on canvas board 41 x 51 cm 1976

Three miles in three heats: — Ah, my sonny,
  The horses in those days were stout,
They had to run well to win money;
  I don't see such horses about.
Your six-furlong vermin that scamper
  Half-a-mile with their feather-weight up,
They wouldn't earn much of their damper
  In a race like the President's Cup.

The first heat was soon set a-going;
  The Dancer went off to the front;
The Don on his quarters was showing,
  With Pardon right out of the hunt.
He rolled and he weltered and wallowed —
  You'd kick your hat faster, I'll bet;
They finished all bunched, and he followed
  All lathered and dripping with sweat.

But troubles came thicker upon us,
  For while we were rubbing him dry
The stewards came over to warn us:
  "We hear you are running a bye!
If Pardon don't spiel like tarnation
  And win the next heat — if he can —
He'll earn a disqualification;
  Just think over *that* now, my man!"

Our money all gone and our credit,
  Our horse couldn't gallop a yard;
And then people thought that *we* did it
  It really was terribly hard.
We were objects of mirth and derision
  To folks in the lawn and the stand,
And the yells of the clever division
  Of "Any price Pardon!" were grand.

We still had a chance for the money,
  Two heats still remained to be run:
If both fell to us — why, my sonny,
  The clever division were done.
And Pardon was better, we reckoned,
  His sickness was passing away,
So we went to the post for the second
  And principal heat of the day.

They're off and away with a rattle,
  Like dogs from the leashes let slip,
And right at the back of the battle
  He followed them under the whip.
They gained ten good lengths on him quickly
  He dropped right away from the pack;
I tell you it made me feel sickly
  To see the blue jacket fall back.

Our very last hope had departed —
  We thought the old fellow was done,
When all of a sudden he started
  To go like a shot from a gun.
His chances seemed slight to embolden
  Our hearts; but, with teeth firmly set,
We thought, "Now or never! The old un
  May reckon with some of 'em yet."

Then loud rose the war-cry from Pardon;
  He swept like the wind down the dip,
And over the rise by the garden
  The jockey was done with the whip.
The field was at sixes and sevens —
  The pace at the first had been fast —
And hope seemed to drop from the heavens,
  For Pardon was coming at last.

And how he did come! It was splendid;
  He gained on them yards every bound,
Stretching out like a greyhound extended,
  His girth laid right down on the ground.
A shimmer of silk in the cedars
  As into the running they wheeled,
And out flashed the whips on the leaders,
  For Pardon had collared the field.

Then right through the ruck he was sailing —
  I knew that the battle was won —
The son of Haphazard was failing,
  The Yattendon filly was done;
He cut down The Don and The Dancer,
  He raced clean away from the mare —
He's in front! Catch him now if you can, sir!
  And up went my hat in the air!

Then loud from the lawn and the garden
   Rose offers of "Ten to one *on!*"
"Who'll bet on the field? I back Pardon!"
   No use; all the money was gone.
He came for the third heat light-hearted,
   A-jumping and dancing about;
The others were done ere they started
   Crestfallen, and tired, and worn out.

He won it, and ran it much faster
   Than even the first, I believe;
Oh, he was the daddy, the master,
   Was Pardon, the son of Reprieve.
He showed 'em the method of travel —
   The boy sat still as a stone —
They never could see him for gravel;
   He came in hard-held, and alone.

     .   .   .

But he's old — and his eyes are grown hollow
   Like me, with my thatch of the snow;
When he dies, then I hope I may follow,
   And go where the racehorses go.
I don't want no harping nor singing —
   Such things with my style don't agree;
Where the hoofs of the horses are ringing
   There's music sufficient for me.

And surely the thoroughbred horses
   Will rise up again and begin
Fresh races on far-away courses,
   And p'raps they might let me slip in.
It would look rather well the race-card on
   'Mongst Cherubs and Seraphs and things,
"Angel Harrison's black gelding Pardon,
   Blue halo, white body and wings."

And if they have racing hereafter,
   (And who is to say they will not?)
When the cheers and the shouting and laughter
   Proclaim that the battle grows hot;
As they come down the racecourse a-steering,
   He'll rush to the front, I believe;
And you'll hear the great multitude cheering
   For Pardon, the son of Reprieve.

OLD PARDON, THE SON OF REPRIEVE III
Oil on hardboard 35 x 45 cm 1976

"Shouting" for a Camel

IT was over at Coolgardie that a mining speculator,
  Who was going down the township just to make a bit o' chink,
Went off to hire a camel from a camel propagator,
  And the Afghan said he'd lend it if he'd stand the beast a drink.
Yes, the only price he asked him was to stand the beast a drink.
He was cheap, very cheap, as the dromedaries go.

So the mining speculator made the bargain, proudly thinking
  He had bested old Mahomet, he had done him in the eye.
Then he clambered on the camel, and the while the beast was
    drinking
  He explained with satisfaction to the miners standing by
That 'twas cheap, very cheap, as the dromedaries go.

But the camel kept on drinking and he filled his hold with water,
  And the more he had inside him yet the more he seemed to need;
For he drank it by the gallon, and his girths grew taut and tauter,
  And the miners muttered softly, "Yes he's very dry indeed!
But he's cheap, very cheap, as the dromedaries go."

So he drank up twenty buckets — it was weird to watch him suck it,
  (And the market price for water was per bucket half-a-crown)
Till the speculator stopped him, saying, "Not another bucket —
  If I give him any more there'll be a famine in the town.
Take him back to old Mahomet, and I'll tramp it through the
    town."
He was cheap, very cheap, as the speculators go.

There's a moral to this story — in your hat you ought to paste it —
  Be careful whom you shout for when a camel is about,
And there's plenty human camels who, before they'll see you
    waste it,
  Will drink up all you pay for if you're fool enough to shout;
If you chance to strike a camel when you're fool enough to shout,
You'll be cheap, very cheap, as the speculators go.

"SHOUTING" FOR A CAMEL
Oil on hardboard 35 x 45 cm 1976

Pioneers

THEY came of bold and roving stock that would not fixed abide;
They were the sons of field and flock since e'er they learnt to ride,
We may not hope to see such men in these degenerate years
As those explorers of the bush — the brave old pioneers.

'Twas they who rode the trackless bush in heat and storm and
    drought;
'Twas they who heard the master-word that called them farther
    out;
'Twas they who followed up the trail the mountain cattle made,
And pressed across the mighty range where now their bones are laid.

But now the times are dull and slow, the brave old days are dead
When hardy bushmen started out, and forced their way ahead
By tangled scrub and forests grim towards the unknown west,
And spied at last the promised land from off the range's crest.

O ye that sleep in lonely graves by distant ridge and plain,
We drink to you in silence now as Christmas comes again,
To you who fought the wilderness through rough unsettled years —
The founders of our nation's life, the brave old pioneers.

PIONEERS
Oil on hardboard 35 x 49 cm 1976

The Man Who Was Away

THE widow sought the lawyer's room with children three in tow,
She told the lawyer man her tale in tones of deepest woe.
She said, "My husband took to drink for pains in his inside,
And never drew a sober breath from then until he died.

"He never drew a sober breath, he died without a will,
And I must sell the bit of land the childer's mouths to fill.
There's some is grown and gone away, but some is childer yet,
And times is very bad indeed — a livin's hard to get.

"There's Min and Sis and little Chris, they stops at home with me,
And Sal has married Greenhide Bill that breaks for Bidgeree.
And Fred is drovin' Conroy's sheep along the Castlereagh
And Charley's shearin' down the Bland, and Peter is away."

The lawyer wrote the details down in ink of legal blue —
"There's Minnie, Susan, Christopher, they stop at home with you;
There's Sarah, Frederick, and Charles, I'll write to them today,
But what about the other son — the one who is away?

"You'll have to furnish his consent to sell the bit of land."
The widow shuffled in her seat, "Oh, don't you understand?
I thought a lawyer ought to know — I don't know what to say —
You'll have to do without him, boss, for Peter is away."

But here the little boy spoke up — said he, "We thought you knew;
He's done six months in Goulburn gaol — he's got six more to do."
Thus in one comprehensive flash he made it clear as day,
The mystery of Peter's life — the man who was away.

THE MAN WHO WAS AWAY
Oil on hardboard 35 x 45 cm 1976

The Open Steeplechase

I HAD ridden over hurdles up the country once or twice,
By the side of Snowy River with a horse they called "The Ace".
And we brought him down to Sydney, and our rider, Jimmy Rice,
Got a fall and broke his shoulder, so they nabbed me in a trice —
Me, that never wore the colours, for the Open Steeplechase.

"Make the running," said the trainer, "it's your only chance
     whatever,
Make it hot from start to finish, for the old black horse can stay,
And just think of how they'll take it, when they hear on Snowy
     River
That the country boy was plucky, and the country horse was
     clever.
You must ride for old Monaro and the mountain boys today."

"Are you ready?" said the starter, as we held the horses back.
All ablazing with impatience, with excitement all aglow;
Before us like a ribbon stretched the steeplechasing track,
And the sun-rays glistened brightly on the chestnut and the black
As the starter's words came slowly, "Are — you — ready? Go!"

Well I scarcely knew we'd started, I was stupid-like with wonder
Till the field closed up beside me and a jump appeared ahead.
And we flew it like a hurdle, not a baulk and not a blunder,
As we charged it all together, and it fairly whistled under,
And then some were pulled behind me and a few shot out and led.

So we ran for half the distance, and I'm making no pretences
When I tell you I was feeling very nervous-like and queer,
For those jockeys rode like demons; you would think they'd lost
     their senses
If you saw them rush their horses at those rasping five-foot fences —
And in place of making running I was falling to the rear.

Till a chap came racing past me on a horse they called "The
     Quiver",
And said he, "My country joker, are you going to give it best?
Are you frightened of the fences? does their stoutness make you
     shiver?
Have they come to breeding cowards by the side of Snowy River?
Are there riders on Monaro? — " but I never heard the rest.

THE OPEN STEEPLECHASE I
Oil on hardboard 35 x 45 cm 1976

For I drove The Ace and sent him just as fast as he could pace it
At the big black line of timber stretching fair across the track,
And he shot beside The Quiver. "Now," said I, "my boy, we'll
    race it.
You can come with Snowy River if you're only game to face it,
Let us mend the pace a little and we'll see who cries a crack."

So we raced away together, and we left the others standing,
And the people cheered and shouted as we settled down to ride,
And we clung beside The Quiver. At his taking off and landing
I could see his scarlet nostril and his mighty ribs expanding,
And The Ace stretched out in earnest, and we held him stride
    for stride.

But the pace was so terrific that they soon ran out their tether —
They were rolling in their gallop, they were fairly blown and
    beat —
But they both were game as pebbles — neither one would show the
    feather.
And we rushed them at the fences, and they cleared them both
    together,
Nearly every time they clouted, but they somehow kept their feet.

Then the last jump rose before us, and they faced it game as
    ever —
We were both at spur and whipcord, fetching blood at every
    bound —
And above the people's cheering and the cries of "Ace" and "Quiver',
I could hear the trainer shouting, "One more run for Snowy River."
Then we struck the jump together and came smashing to the
    ground.

Well, The Quiver ran to blazes, but The Ace stood still and
    waited,
Stood and waited like a statue while I scrambled on his back.
There was no one next or near me for the field was fairly slated,
So I cantered home a winner with my shoulder dislocated,
While the man who rode The Quiver followed limping down the
    track.

And he shook my hand and told me that in all his days he never
Met a man who rode more gamely, and our last set-to was prime.
Then we wired them on Monaro how we chanced to beat The
    Quiver,
And they sent us back an answer, "Good old sort from Snowy
    River:
Send us word each race you start in and we'll back you every
    time."

THE OPEN STEEPLECHASE II
Oil on hardboard 35 x 45 cm 1976

The Last Trump

"You led the trump," the old man said
  With fury in his eye,
"And yet you hope my girl to wed!
Young man! your hopes of love are fled,
  'Twere better she should die!

"My sweet young daughter sitting there,
  So innocent and plump!
You don't suppose that she would care
To wed an outlawed man who'd dare
  To lead the thirteenth trump!

"If you had drawn their leading spade
  It meant a certain win!
But no! By Pembroke's mighty shade
The thirteenth trump you went and played
  And let their diamonds in!

"My girl, return at my command
  His presents in a lump!
Return his ring! For, understand,
No man is fit to hold your hand
  Who leads a thirteenth trump!

"But hold! Give every man his due
  And every dog his day.
Speak up and say what made you do
This dreadful thing — that is, if you
  Have anything to say!"

He spoke. "I meant at first," said he,
  "To give their spades a bump,
Or lead the hearts; but then you see
I thought against us there might be,
  Perhaps, a fourteenth trump!"

      .   .   .

They buried him at dawn of day
  Beside a ruined stump:
And there he sleeps the hours away
And waits for Gabriel to play
  The last — the fourteenth trump.

THE LAST TRUMP
Oil on hardboard 39 x 45 cm 1976

The Flying Gang

I SERVED my time, in the days gone by,
  In the railway's clash and clang,
And I worked my way to the end, and I
  Was the head of the "Flying Gang".
'Twas a chosen band that was kept at hand
  In case of an urgent need;
Was it south or north, we were started forth
  And away at our utmost speed.
If word reached town that a bridge was down,
  The imperious summons rang —
"Come out with the pilot engine sharp,
  And away with the flying gang."

Then a piercing scream and a rush of steam
  As the engine moved ahead;
With measured beat by the slum and street
  Of the busy town we fled,
By the uplands bright and the homesteads white,
  With the rush of the western gale —
And the pilot swayed with the pace we made
  As she rocked on the ringing rail.
And the country children clapped their hands
  As the engine's echoes rang.
But their elders said: "There is work ahead
  When they send for the flying gang."

Then across the miles of the saltbush plain
  That gleamed with the morning dew,
Where the grasses waved like the ripening grain
  The pilot engine flew —
A fiery rush in the open bush
  Where the grade marks seemed to fly,
And the order sped on the wires ahead,
  The pilot *must* go by.
The Governor's special must stand aside,
  And the fast express go hang;
Let your orders be that the line is free
  For the boys of the flying gang.

THE FLYING GANG
Oil on hardboard 35 x 45 cm 1976

How M'Ginnis Went Missing

LET us cease our idle chatter,
    Let the tears bedew our cheek,
For a man from Tallangatta
    Has been missing for a week.

Where the roaring flooded Murray
    Covered all the lower land,
There he started in a hurry,
    With a bottle in his hand.

And his fate is hid for ever,
    But the public seem to think
That he slumbered by the river,
    'Neath the influence of drink.

And they scarcely seem to wonder
    That the river, wide and deep,
Never woke him with its thunder,
    Never stirred him in his sleep.

As the crashing logs came sweeping
    And their tumult filled the air,
Then M'Ginnis murmured, sleeping,
    "'Tis a wake in ould Kildare."

So the river rose and found him
    Sleeping softly by the stream.
And the cruel waters drowned him
    Ere he wakened from his dream.

And the blossom-tufted wattle,
    Blooming brightly on the lea,
Saw M'Ginnis and the bottle
    Going drifting out to sea.

HOW M'GINNIS WENT MISSING
Oil on hardboard 40 x 30 cm 1976

Last Week

Oh, the new chum went to the backblock run,
But he should have gone there last week.
He tramped ten miles with a loaded gun,
But of turkey or duck saw never a one,
For he should have been there last week,
   They said,
There were flocks of 'em there last week.

He wended his way to a waterfall,
And he should have gone there last week.
He carried a camera, legs and all,
But the day was hot and the stream was small,
For he should have gone there last week,
   They said,
They drowned a man there last week.

He went for a drive, and he made a start,
Which should have been made last week,
For the old horse died of a broken heart;
So he footed it home and he dragged the cart —
But the horse was all right last week,
   They said,
He trotted a match last week.

So he asked the bushies who came from afar
To visit the town last week
If they'd dine with him, and they said "Hurrah!"
But there wasn't a drop in the whisky jar —
You should have been here last week,
   He said,
I drank it all up last week!

LAST WEEK
Oil on hardboard 35 x 45 cm 1976

Saltbush Bill's Gamecock

'TWAS Saltbush Bill, with his travelling sheep, was making his way
    to town;
He crossed them over the Hard Times Run, and he came to the
    Take 'Em Down;
He counted through at the boundary gate, and camped at the
    drafting yard:
For Stingy Smith, of the Hard Times Run, had hunted him rather
    hard.
He bore no malice to Stingy Smith — 'twas simply the hand of Fate
That caused his waggon to swerve aside and shatter old Stingy's gate;
And being only the hand of Fate, it follows, without a doubt,
It wasn't the fault of Saltbush Bill that Stingy's sheep got out.
So Saltbush Bill, with an easy heart, prepared for what might befall,
Commenced his stages on Take 'Em Down, the station of Rooster
    Hall.

'Tis strange how often the men out back will take to some curious
    craft,
Some ruling passion to keep their thoughts away from the overdraft;
And Rooster Hall, of the Take 'Em Down, was widely known to
    fame
As breeder of champion fighting cocks — his *forte* was the British
    Game.

The passing stranger within his gates that camped with old Rooster
    Hall
Was forced to talk about fowls all night, or else not talk at all.
Though droughts should come, and though sheep should die, his
    fowls were his sole delight;
He left his shed in the flood of work to watch two gamecocks fight.
He held in scorn the Australian Game, that long-legged child of sin;
In a desperate fight, with the steel-tipped spurs, the British game
    must win!
The Australian bird was a mongrel bird, with a touch of the
    jungle cock;
The want of breeding must find him out, when facing the English
    stock;
For British breeding, and British pluck, must triumph it over all —
And that was the root of the simple creed that governed old
    Rooster Hall.

.   .   .   .   .   .

SALTBUSH BILL'S GAMECOCK I
Oil on hardboard 40 x 50 cm 1976

'Twas Saltbush Bill to the station rode ahead of his travelling
    sheep,
And sent a message to Rooster Hall that wakened him out of his
    sleep —
A crafty message that fetched him out, and hurried him as he
    came —
"A drover has an Australian bird to match with your British Game."
'Twas done, and done in half a trice; a five-pound note a side;
Old Rooster Hall, with his champion bird, and the drover's bird
    untried.

"Steel spurs, of course?" said old Rooster Hall; "you'll need 'em
    without a doubt!"
"You stick the spurs on your bird!" said Bill, "but mine fights best
    without."
"Fights best without?" said old Rooster Hall; "he can't fight best
    unspurred!
You must be crazy!" But Saltbush Bill said, "Wait till you see my
    bird!"
So Rooster Hall to his fowl-yard went, and quickly back he came,
Bearing a clipt and a shaven cock, the pride of his English Game;
With an eye as fierce as an eaglehawk, and a crow like a trumpet
    call,
He strutted about on the garden walk, and cackled at Rooster
    Hall.
Then Rooster Hall sent off a boy with a word to his cronies two,
McCrae (the boss of the Black Police) and Father Donahoo.

Full many a cockfight old McCrae had held in his empty Court,
With Father D. as the picker-up — a regular all-round Sport!
They got the message of Rooster Hall, and down to his run they
    came,
Prepared to scoff at the drover's bird, and to bet on the English
    Game;
They hied them off to the drover's camp, while Saltbush rode
    before —
Old Rooster Hall was a blithsome man, when he thought of the
    treat in store.
They reached the camp, where the drover's cook, with countenance
    all serene,
Was boiling beef in an iron pot, but never a fowl was seen.

SALTBUSH BILL'S GAMECOCK II
Oil on hardboard 35 x 45 cm 1976

"Take off the beef from the fire," said Bill, "and wait till you see
    the fight;
There's something fresh for the bill-of-fare — there's game-fowl stew
    tonight!
For Mister Hall has a fighting cock, all feathered and clipped and
    spurred;
And he's fetched him here, for a bit of sport, to fight our Australian
    bird.
I've made a match that our pet will win, though he's hardly a
    fighting cock,
But he's game enough, and it's many a mile that he's tramped with
    the travelling stock."
The cook he banged on a saucepan lid; and, soon as the sound was
    heard,
Under the dray, in the shallow hid, a something moved and
    stirred:
A great tame emu strutted out. Said Saltbush, "Here's our bird!"
But Rooster Hall, and his cronies two, drove home without a
    word.

The passing stranger within his gates that camps with old Rooster
    Hall
Must talk about something else than fowls, if he wishes to talk
    at all.
For the record lies in the local Court, and filed in its deepest vault,
That Peter Hall, of the Take 'Em Down, was tried for a fierce
    assault
On a stranger man, who, in all good faith, and prompted by what
    he heard,
Had asked old Hall if a British Game could beat an Australian bird;
And Old McCrae, who was on the Bench as soon as the case
    was tried,
Remarked, "Discharged with a clean discharge — the assault was
    justified!"

SALTBUSH BILL'S GAMECOCK III
Oil on hardboard 40 x 49 cm 1976

A Bushman's Song

I'M travelling down the Castlereagh, and I'm a station-hand,
I'm handy with the ropin' pole, I'm handy with the brand,
And I can ride a rowdy colt, or swing the axe all day,
But there's no demand for a station-hand along the Castlereagh.

So it's shift, boys, shift, for there isn't the slightest doubt
That we've got to make a shift to the stations further out,
With the pack-horse runnin' after, for he follows like a dog,
We must strike across the country at the old jig-jog.

This old black horse I'm riding — if you'll notice what's his brand,
He wears the crooked R, you see — none better in the land.
He takes a lot of beatin', and the other day we tried,
For a bit of a joke, with a racing bloke, for twenty pound a side.

It was shift, boys, shift, for there wasn't the slightest doubt
That I had to make him shift, for the money was nearly out,
But he cantered home a winner, with the other one at the flog —
He's a red-hot sort to pick up with his old jig-jog.

I asked a cove for shearin' once along the Marthaguy:
"We shear non-union here," says he. "I call it scab," says I.
I looked along the shearin' floor before I turned to go —
There were eight or ten dashed Chinamen a-shearin' in a row.

It was shift, boys, shift, for there wasn't the slightest doubt
It was time to make a shift with the leprosy about.
So I saddled up my horses, and I whistled to my dog,
And I left his scabby station at the old jig-jog.

I went to Illawarra, where my brother's got a farm;
He has to ask his landlord's leave before he lifts his arm:
The landlord owns the country-side — man, woman, dog, and cat,
They haven't the cheek to dare to speak without they touch their hat.

It was shift, boys, shift, for there wasn't the slightest doubt
Their little landlord god and I would soon have fallen out,
Was I to touch my hat to him? — was I his bloomin' dog?
So I makes for up the country at the old jig-jog.

A BUSHMAN'S SONG
Oil on hardboard 35 x 45 cm 1976

But it's time that I was movin', I've a mighty way to go
Till I drink artesian water from a thousand feet below;
Till I meet the overlanders with the cattle comin' down —
And I'll work a while till I make a pile, then have a spree in town.

So it's shift, boys, shift, for there isn't the slightest doubt
We've got to make a shift to the stations further ou'
The pack-horse runs behind us, for he follows like a dog,
And we cross a lot of country at the old jig-jog.

Father Riley's Horse

'TWAS the horse thief, Andy Regan, that was hunted like a dog
  By the troopers of the Upper Murray side;
They had searched in every gully, they had looked in every log
  But never sight or track of him they spied,
Till the priest at Kiley's Crossing heard a knocking very late
  And a whisper "Father Riley — come across!"
So his Reverence, in pyjamas, trotted softly to the gate
  And admitted Andy Regan — and a horse!

"Now, it's listen, Father Riley, to the words I've got to say,
  For it's close upon the death I am tonight.
With the troopers hard behind me I've been hiding all the day
  In the gullies keeping close and out of sight.
But they're watching all the ranges till there's not a bird could fly,
  And I'm fairly worn to pieces with the strife,
So I'm taking no more trouble, but I'm going home to die,
  'Tis the only way I see to save my life.

"Yes, I'm making home to mother's, and I'll die o' Tuesday next
  An' buried on the Thursday — and, of course,
I'm prepared to do my penance; but with one thing I'm perplexed
  And it's — Father, it's this jewel of a horse!
He was never bought nor paid for, and there's not a man can
    swear
  To his owner or his breeder, but I know
That his sire was by Pedantic from the Old Pretender mare,
  And his dam was close related to The Roe.

"And there's nothing in the district that can race him for a step —
  He could canter while they're going at their top:
He's the king of all the leppers that was ever seen to lep;
  A five-foot fence — he'd clear it in a hop!
So I'll leave him with you, Father, till the dead shall rise again,
  'Tis yourself that knows a good un; and, of course,
You can say he's got by Moonlight out of Paddy Murphy's plain
  If you're ever asked the breeding of the horse!

"But it's getting on to daylight, and it's time to say good-bye,
  For the stars above the East are growing pale.
And I'm making home to mother — and it's hard for me to die!
  But it's harder still, is keeping out of gaol!
You can ride the old horse over to my grave across the dip,
  Where the wattle-bloom is waving overhead.
Sure he'll jump them fences easy — you must never raise the whip
  Or he'll rush 'em! — now, good-bye!" and he had fled!

So they buried Andy Regan, and they buried him to rights,
    In the graveyard at the back of Kiley's Hill;
There were five-and-twenty mourners who had five-and-twenty fights
    Till the very boldest fighters had their fill.
There were fifty horses racing from the graveyard to the pub.
    And the riders flogged each other all the while —
And the lashins of the liquor! And the lavins of the grub!
    Oh, poor Andy went to rest in proper style.

Then the races came to Kiley's — with a steeple chase and all,
    For the folk were mostly Irish round about,
And it takes an Irish rider to be fearless of a fall;
    They were training morning in and morning out.
But they never started training till the sun was on the course,
    For a superstitious story kept 'em back.
That the ghost of Andy Regan on a slashing chestnut horse
    Had been training by the starlight on the track.

And they read the nominations for the races with surprise
    And amusement at the Father's little joke,
For a novice had been entered for the steeplechasing prize,
    And they found that it was Father Riley's moke!
He was neat enough to gallop, he was strong enough to stay!
    But his owner's views of training were immense,
For the Reverend Father Riley used to ride him every day,
    And he never saw a hurdle nor a fence.

And the priest would join the laughter, "Oh," said he, "I put him in,
    For there's five-and-twenty sovereigns to be won;
And the poor would find it useful if the chestnut chanced to win.
    As he'll maybe do when all is said and done!"
He had called him Faugh-a-ballagh (which is French for 'Clear
    the course'),
    And his colours were a vivid shade of green:
All the Dooleys and O'Donnells were on Father Riley's horse,
    While the Orangeman were backing Mandarin!

It was Hogan, the dog-poisoner — aged man and very wise,
    Who was camping in the racecourse with his swag,
And who ventured the opinion, to the township's great surprise,
    That the race would go to Father Riley's nag.
"You can talk about your riders — and the horse has not been
    schooled,
    And the fences is terrific, and the rest!
When the field is fairly going, then ye'll see ye've all been fooled.
    And the chestnut horse will battle with the best.

FATHER RILEY'S HORSE I
Oil on hardboard 40 x 50 cm 1976

"For there's some has got condition, and they think the race is
  sure,
    And the chestnut horse will fall beneath the weight;
But the hopes of all the helpless, and the prayers of all the poor,
    Will be running by his side to keep him straight.
And it's what the need of schoolin' or of workin' on the track,
    Whin the Saints are there to guide him round the course!
I've prayed him over every fence — I've prayed him out and back!
    And I'll bet my cash on Father Riley's horse!"

     .   .   .   .   .   .

Oh, the steeple was a caution! They went tearin' round and round,
    And the fences rang and rattled where they struck.
There was some that cleared the water — there was more fell in and
  drowned —
    Some blamed the men and others blamed the luck!
But the whips were flying freely when the field came into view
    For the finish down the long green stretch of course,
And in front of all the flyers, jumpin' like a kangaroo,
    Came the rank outsider — Father Riley's horse!

Oh, the shouting and the cheering as he rattled past the post!
    For he left the others standing, in the straight;
And the rider — well, they reckoned it was Andy Regan's ghost,
    And it beat 'em how a ghost would draw the weight!
But he weighed in, nine stone seven; then he laughed and dis-
  appeared,
    Like a Banshee (which is Spanish for an elf),
And old Hogan muttered sagely, "If it wasn't for the beard
    They'd be thinking it was Andy Regan's self!"

And the poor at Kiley's Crossing drank the health at Christmastide
    Of the chestnut and his rider dressed in green.
There was never such a rider, not since Andy Regan died,
    And they wondered who on earth he could have been,
But they settled it amongst 'em, for the story got about,
    'Mongst the bushmen and the people on the course,
That the Devil had been ordered to let Andy Regan out
    For the steeplechase on Father Riley's horse!

FATHER RILEY'S HORSE II
Oil on hardboard 35 x 45 cm 1976

Riders in the Stand

THERE's some that ride the Robbo style, and bump at every stride;
While others sit a long way back, to get a longer ride.
There's some that ride as sailors do, with legs, and arms, and teeth;
And some ride on the horse's neck, and some ride underneath.

But all the finest horsemen out — the men to Beat the Band —
You'll find amongst the crowd that ride their races in the Stand.
They'll say "He had the race in hand, and lost it in the straight."
They'll show how Godby came too soon, and Barden came too late.

They'll say Chevalley lost his nerve, and Regan lost his head;
They'll tell how one was "livened up" and something else was
    "dead" —
In fact, the race was never run on sea, or sky, or land,
But what you'd get it better done by riders in the Stand.

The rule holds good in everything in life's uncertain fight;
You'll find the winner can't go wrong, the loser can't go right.
You ride a slashing race, and lose — by one and all you're banned!
Ride like a bag of flour, and win — they'll cheer you in the Stand.

RIDERS IN THE STAND
Oil on hardboard 35 x 45 cm 1976

Bottle-O!

I AIN'T the kind of bloke as takes to any steady job;
  I drives me bottle cart around the town;
A bloke what keeps 'is eyes about can always make a bob —
  I couldn't bear to graft for every brown.
There's lots of handy things about in everybody's yard,
  There's cocks and hens a-running' to an' fro,
And little dogs what comes and barks — we take 'em off their guard
  And we puts 'em with the Empty Bottle-O!

Chorus —

So it's any "Empty bottles! Any empty bottle-O!"
You can hear us round for half a mile or so.
    And you'll see the women rushing
    To take in the Monday's washing
When they 'ear us crying, "Empty Bottle-O!"

I'm driving down by Wexford-street and up a winder goes,
  A girl sticks out 'er 'ead and looks at me,
An all-right tart with ginger 'air, and freckles on 'er nose;
  I stops the cart and walks across to see.
"There ain't no bottles 'ere," says she, "since father took the pledge,"
  "No bottles 'ere," says I, "I'd like to know
What right 'ave you to stick your 'ead outside the winder ledge,
  If you 'aven't got no Empty Bottle-O!"

I sometimes gives the 'orse a spell, and then the push and me
  We takes a little trip to Chowder Bay.
Oh! ain't it nice the 'ole day long a-gazin' at the sea
  And a-hidin' of the tanglefoot away.
But when the booze gits 'old of us, and fellows starts to "scrap",
  There's some what likes blue-metal for to throw:
But as for me, I always says for layin' out a "trap"
  There's nothing like an Empty Bottle-O!

BOTTLE-O!
Oil on hardboard 35 x 45 cm 1976

Story of Mongrel Grey

THIS is the story the stockman told
  On the cattle-camp, when the stars were bright;
The moon rose up like a globe of gold
  And flooded the plain with her mellow light.
    We watched the cattle till dawn of day
    And he told me the story of Mongrel Grey.

He was a knock-about station hack,
  Spurred and walloped, and banged and beat;
Ridden all day with a sore on his back,
  Left all night with nothing to eat.
    That was a matter of everyday
    Normal occurrence with Mongrel Grey.

We might have sold him, but someone heard
  He was bred out back on a flooded run,
Where he learnt to swim like a waterbird;
  Midnight or midday were all as one —
    In the flooded ground he would find his way;
    Nothing could puzzle old Mongrel Grey.

'Tis a trick, no doubt, that some horses learn;
  When the floods are out they will splash along
In girth-deep water, and twist and turn
  From hidden channel and billabong,
    Never mistaking the road to go;
    For a man may guess — but the horses *know*.

I was camping out with my youngest son —
  Bit of a nipper, just learnt to speak —
In an empty hut on the lower run,
  Shooting and fishing in Conroy's Creek.
    The youngster toddled about all day
    And there with our horses was Mongrel Grey.

All of a sudden a flood came down,
  At first a freshet of mountain rain,
Roaring and eddying, rank and brown,
  Over the flats and across the plain.
    Rising and rising — at fall of night
    Nothing but water appeared in sight!

STORY OF MONGREL GREY
Oil on hardboard 35 x 45 cm 1976

'Tis a nasty place when the floods are out,
　　Even in daylight; for all around
Channels and billabongs twist about,
　　Stretching for miles in the flooded ground.
　　　　And to move seemed a hopeless thing to try
　　　　In the dark with the storm-water racing by.

I had to risk it. I heard a roar
　　As the wind swept down and the driving rain;
And the water rose till it reached the floor
　　Of our highest room; and 'twas very plain —
　　　　The way the torrent was sweeping down —
　　　　We must make for the highlands at once, or drown.

Off to the stable I splashed, and found
　　The horses shaking with cold and fright;
I led them down to the lower ground,
　　But never a yard would they swim that night!
　　　　They reared and snorted and turned away,
　　　　And none would face it but Mongrel Grey.

I bound the child on the horse's back,
　　And we started off, with a prayer to heaven,
Through the rain and the wind and the pitchy black
　　For I knew that the instinct God has given
　　　　To prompt His creatures by night and day
　　　　Would guide the footsteps of Mongrel Grey.

He struck deep water at once and swam —
　　I swam beside him and held his mane —
Till we touched the bank of the broken dam
　　In shallow water; then off again,
　　　　Swimming in darkness across the flood,
　　　　Rank with the smell of the drifting mud.

He turned and twisted across and back,
　　Choosing the places to wade or swim,
Picking the safest and shortest track —
　　The blackest darkness was clear to him.
　　　　Did he strike the crossing by sight or smell?
　　　　The Lord that held him alone could tell!

He dodged the timber whene'er he could,
  But timber brought us to grief at last;
I was partly stunned by a log of wood
  That struck my head as it drifted past;
    Then lost my grip of the brave old grey,
    And in half a second he swept away.

I reached a tree, where I had to stay,
  And did a perish for two day's hard;
And lived on water — but Mongrel Grey,
  He walked right into the homestead yard
    At dawn next morning, and grazed around,
    With the child strapped on to him safe and sound.

We keep him now for the wife to ride,
  Nothing too good for him now, of course;
Never a whip on his fat old hide,
  For she owes the child to that brave grey horse.
    And not Old Tyson himself could pay
    The purchase money of Mongrel Grey.

A Mountain Station

I BOUGHT a run a while ago
    On country rough and ridgy,
Where wallaroos and wombats grow —
    The Upper Murrumbidgee.
The grass is rather scant, it's true,
    But this a fair exchange is,
The sheep can see a lovely view
    By climbing up the ranges.

And She-oak Flat's the station's name,
    I'm not surprised at that, sirs:
The oaks were there before I came,
    And I supplied the flat, sirs.
A man would wonder how it's done,
    The stock so soon decreases —
They sometimes tumble off the run
    And break themselves to pieces.

I've tried to make expenses meet,
    But wasted all my labours;
The sheep the dingoes didn't eat
    Were stolen by the neighbours.
They stole my pears — my native pears —
    Those thrice-convicted felons,
And ravished from me unawares
    My crop of paddy-melons.

And sometimes under sunny skies,
    Without an explanation,
The Murrumbidgee used to rise
    And overflow the station.
But this was caused (as now I know)
    When summer sunshine glowing
Had melted all Kiandra's snow
    And set the river going.

Then in the news, perhaps, you read:
    "Stock Passings. Puckawidgee,
Fat cattle: Seven hundred head
    Swept down the Murrumbidgee;
Their destination's quite obscure,
    But, somehow, there's a notion,
Unless the river falls, they're sure
    To reach the Southern Ocean."

A MOUNTAIN STATION I
Oil on hardboard 35 x 45 cm 1976

So after that I'll give it best;
　No more with Fate I'll battle.
I'll let the river take the rest,
　For those were all my cattle.
And with one comprehensive curse
　I close my brief narration,
And advertise it in my verse —
　"For Sale! A Mountain Station."

A MOUNTAIN STATION II
Oil on hardboard 35 x 45 cm 1976

Jim Carew

Born of a thoroughbred English race,
  Well proportioned and closely knit,
Neat, slim figure and handsome face,
  Always ready and always fit,
Hardy and wiry of limb and thew,
That was the ne'er-do-well Jim Carew.

One of the sons of the good old land —
  Many a year since his like was known;
Never a game but he took command,
  Never a sport but he held his own;
Gained at his college a triple blue —
Good as they make them was Jim Carew.

Came to grief — was it card or horse?
  Nobody asked and nobody cared;
Ship him away to the bush of course,
  Ne'er-do-well fellows are easily spared;
Only of women a sorrowing few
Wept at parting from Jim Carew.

Gentleman Jim on the cattle-camp
  Sitting his horse with an easy grace;
But the reckless living has left its stamp
  In the deep drawn lines of that handsome face,
And the harder look in those eyes of blue:
Prompt at a quarrel is Jim Carew.

Billy the Lasher was out for gore —
  Twelve-stone navvy with chest of hair —
When he opened out with a hungry roar
  On a ten-stone man, it was hardly fair;
But his wife was wise if his face she knew
By the time you were done with him, Jim Carew.

Gentleman Jim in the stockmen's hut
  Works with them, toils with them, side by side;
As to his past — well, his lips are shut.
  "Gentleman once," say his mates with pride,
And the wildest Cornstalk can ne'er outdo
In feats of recklessness Jim Carew.

JIM CAREW
Oil on hardboard 35 x 45 cm 1976

What should he live for? A dull despair!
   Drink is his master and drags him down,
Water of Lethe that drowns all care.
   Gentleman Jim has a lot to drown,
And he reigns as king with a drunken crew,
Sinking to misery, Jim Carew.

Such is the end of the ner'er-do-well —
   Jimmy the Boozer, all down at heel;
But he straightens up when he's asked to tell
   His name and race, and a flash of steel
Still lightens up in those eyes of blue —
"I am, or — no, I *was* — Jim Carew."

The Travelling Post Office

THE roving breezes come and go, the reed-beds sweep and sway,
The sleepy river murmurs low, and loiters on its way,
It is the land of lots o' time along the Castlereagh.

    .   .   .   .

The old man's son had left the farm, he found it dull and slow,
He drifted to the great North-west, where all the rovers go.
"He's gone so long," the old man said; "he's dropped right out
    of mind,
But if you'd write a line to him I'd take it very kind;
He's shearing here and fencing there, a kind of waif and stray —
He's droving now with Conroy's sheep along the Castlereagh.

"The sheep are travelling for the grass, and travelling very slow;
They may be at Mundooran now, or past the Overflow,
Or tramping down the black-soil flats across by Waddiwong
But all those little country towns would send the letter wrong.
The mailman, if he's extra tired, would pass them in his sleep;
It's safest to address the note to 'Care of Conroy's sheep',
For five and twenty thousand head can scarcely go astray,
You write to 'Care of Conroy's sheep along the Castlereagh'."

    .   .   .   .

By rock and ridge and riverside the western mail has gone
Across the great Blue Mountain Range to take that letter on.
A moment on the topmost grade, while open fire-doors glare,
She pauses like a living thing to breathe the mountain air,
Then launches down the other side across the plains away
To bear that note to "Conroy's sheep along the Castlereagh".

And now by coach and mailman's bag it goes from town to town,
And Conroy's Gap and Conroy's Creek have marked it "Further
    down".
Beneath a sky of deepest blue, where never cloud abides,
A speck upon the waste of plain the lonely mailman rides.
Where fierce hot winds have set the pine and myall boughs
      asweep
He hails the shearers passing by for news of Conroy's sheep.
By big lagoons where wildfowl play and crested pigeons flock,
By camp-fires where the drovers ride around their restless stock,
And past the teamster toiling down to fetch the wool away
My letter chases Conroy's sheep along the Castlereagh.

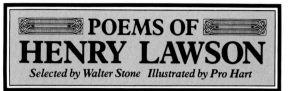

POEMS OF
HENRY LAWSON

Selected by Walter Stone   Illustrated by Pro Hart

SWEENEY II
Oil on hardboard 45 cm × 35 cm 1975

POEMS OF HENRY LAWSON

Selected by Walter Stone   Illustrated by Pro Hart

NH
NEW
HOLLAND

Published by
New Holland Publishers (Australia) Pty Ltd
Sydney • Auckland • London • Cape Town

1/66 Gibbes Street Chatswood NSW 2067 Australia
218 Lake Road Northcote Auckland New Zealand
86 Edgware Road London W2 2EA United Kingdom
80 McKenzie Street Cape Town 8001 South Africa

First published by Lansdowne Press 1982
Reprinted 1983, 1984, 1987, 1988
Reprinted by Weldon Publishing 1991
Reprinted by Ure Smith Press 1992
Reprinted by New Holland Publishers 2007, 2010, 2011

A record of this book is held at the National Library of Australia

9781742571119

Publisher: Fiona Schultz
Publishing Manager: Lliane Clarke
Designer: Emma Gough
Production Manager: Olga Dementiev
Printer: Toppan Leefung Printing (China) Ltd

10 9 8 7 6 5 4 3 2

Contents

"DEAD DUGGAN" FROM TALBRAGAR
Oil on hardboard 45 cm × 35 cm 1975

Introduction

In any part of Australia, almost in any company, the mere mention of Henry Lawson's name will bring an immediate response. Whether it gives rise to an anecdote or a recitation of a few lines of his verse or leads to a discussion of his place in Australian literature it will not pass unnoticed. Alone among our writers he takes his place not only as a writer but as part of the wide Australian tradition.

Few writers in their own time have been so popularly acclaimed and it may be argued that the unqualified adulation led indirectly to his later personal problems. In the literary world, as in all other walks of life, success fans the embers of jealousy and there were not wanting those who saw in his work the faults they failed to find in their own. If, as he did sometimes, smart under their attacks he fought back in caustic verse or prose, time proving him right. His work continues to excite, in different ways, each generation of readers.

The broad outlines of Henry Lawson's biography are now reasonably well documented but much minor detail, vital if we are to have a clear picture of his life and times, remains a blend of fact and fiction which only the intensive research of scholars such as Professor Colin Roderick will sort out. Contradictions and absurdities abound in much that has already been published and will continue to turn up as hitherto unpublished sources such as the private correspondence of his friends and others become available.

So realistically did Lawson identify himself with the times, and the people and the places of which he wrote that it is all too easy to assume that he was indulging in covert autobiography. Much, for instance, may be read into the poem 'The Wander-Light' or the two parts of his 'Fragment of Autobiography' unless the reader is careful to remember that the naturally creative writer has a license to indulge his fancy.

If it pleased him to claim a gypsy ancestry or to infer that he had been harshly treated by some of his friends, he did so careless of the fact that some day the truth would be known. If the facts of his love affair with Hannah Thornburn have been coloured by his recollection or the imagination of his contemporaries it has to be said that the unhappy, wayward genius that was Henry Lawson is not to be tried on these counts but rather on his achievements as a writer of prose and of verse that gave direction and distinction to an indigenous and national Australian literature.

Henry Lawson was born in a tent on the Weddin Mountains alluvial goldfields near the small town of Grenfell, New South Wales, on 17 June 1867. He was the first child of the marriage of Niels Hertzberg Larsen (later anglicised to Lawson) and Louisa Albury, who had married in July of the previous year.

His father was born into a prominent family at Flademoen, Tromoy, Norway in

1832, and was a man of some education and taste who had been trained in maritime navigation. He left his homeland in 1853 vowing never to return, reputedly because of a blighted romance, and almost three years later turned up at Melbourne, where in company with a shipmate, John Henry William Slee, he deserted his ship to try his luck in the goldrushes. Just how far fortune favoured him in the next twelve years we do not know. About the year 1866 still suffering from gold fever, he arrived at the goldfields at New Pipeclay (now called Eurunderee) where Louisa, a daughter of Henry Albury, a bush worker turned shanty-keeper, was living.

One of a family of six daughters and a son, she had been born in 1848 at Mudgee, had received an education, reasonable for the times, at the local public school where her ability had not passed unnoticed by a teacher who encouraged her love of books. Little is known of the courtship of Louisa by Niels but marriage was a bitter experience for each of them.

The restless Niels, unable to resist the lure of gold, took Louisa to the Grenfell diggings and when, a few months later, his son was born he was registered as Henry Lawson. His father was shown as Peter Lawson, the name by which he was generally known in Australia. There is no record of Henry having been baptised and his occasional use of the second names Hertzberg or Archibald is based on a very dubious legend.

The Lawsons soon afterwards returned to Eurunderee where Peter took up a selection which turned out be very poor country. There he built a cottage of which only the brick chimney still stands, now cared for as a literary shrine.

Henry Lawson was to spend the impressionable years of his childhood here, broken only by a period at Gulgong in 'The Roaring Days' and an occasional holiday with his mother's people in Sydney and Wallerawang. Despite his claim that his home-life was unhappy because of the incompatibility of his parents, his childhood would have differed little from that of many other children in the bush — and the city, too.

If there were 'Ragged Schools' for the children in the poverty stricken areas of Sydney there were no schools in many settled parts of the country and the young Henry Lawson was already nine when a Provisional School, 'The Old Bark School', was opened at Eurunderee in October 1876. He, and one of his younger brothers, were among the first pupils. Peter and Louisa Lawson had played a prominent part in the agitation which resulted in the establishment of the school. The mother had, earlier, inspired in her children an interest in literature by reading to them every night. Lawson recalled that he could barely wait for nightfall to hear the continuation of some of the stories.

About this time Lawson's chronic and incurable deafness became apparent and despite the blame he laid on teachers for his failure as a scholar his affliction must have been a contributing factor.

Later, because of a difference of opinion with John Tierney, the local teacher, Louisa sent Henry to a Roman Catholic School at Mudgee. There he came under the influence of Charles Kevan, a district inspector of schools, who encouraged him in his reading and talked to him of poetry. Dickens, Defoe, Marcus Clarke, Boldrewood, Bret Harte and Poe interested him.

Not yet turned fourteen, Lawson's school days and childhood ended. Peter, having abandoned farming, had for some time been engaged in various building contracts in the district and needed his son's help. It meant that Henry was to spend much of his time away from home learning to become a housepainter, acquiring some skill as a carpenter, and broadening his knowledge of bush life.

In 1883 Louisa and Peter leased the property at Eurunderee and Louisa, her marriage at an end, went to Sydney. In no time she sent for Henry, still working with his father, to join her, hoping no doubt to save him from the aimless life of the average bushworker. Finally she and her family settled at 138 Phillip Street which was to become a meeting place for many of the radicals and reformers of the turbulent 1880s, some of whom were later to become public figures, as Louisa herself did.

In the meantime she had Henry apprenticed to coach-painting at the carriage works of Hudson Brothers, at Clyde, a suburb some distance from the city across which the boy had to walk in the early hours of the morning to catch his train. Thus he came face to face with slum life and the social injustices of the day. He attended night classes in the city after his long working day but failed to matriculate for Sydney University. About the same time he abandoned his apprenticeship, and became a painter's improver.

The influence of the groups among whom his mother and he moved soon showed in his youthful attempts to write militant verse and prose and in 1887 he wrote his first prose article for the *Republican*, a radical weekly in which Louisa had an interest and which she hoped her son would one day edit.

In June 1887 four lines of a poem, initialled H. L., appeared in the 'Answers to Correspondents' column in the *Bulletin* with the advice 'try again'. In the following October, whilst he was in Melbourne undergoing further futile treatment for his deafness, the same paper published his 'Song of the Republic'. By the end of the year two more poems had appeared over Lawson's name with a laudatory note referring to him as a youth of seventeen. He was in fact twenty but it was obvious that his work had caught the eye of J. F. Archibald, editor of the weekly *Bulletin* which, founded in 1880, was already shaping public opinion on a catchcry or slogan of 'Australia for the Australians'.

It encouraged, fostered, published and paid for poetry and prose with a regularity which attracted to its pages a group of writers who were ultimately to be known as 'the *Bulletin* school' and whose literary achievements are now regarded as the beginnings of an indigenous Australian literature.

The purely literary pages of the *Bulletin*, as distinct from the political and other sections, were not many but the quixotic and skilful Archibald kept a close watch over everything that appeared and continually advised and even schooled his contributors in the terse style which he demanded. Lawson was quick to learn and the time was not far ahead when he would be hailed as the most brilliant of the *Bulletin* authors.

Barely twenty-one when 'Faces in the Street' was published, almost overnight he was famous. In a single poem he had exposed socal injustice in stanzas far more inspiring than any leader writer in the daily press could have done. About this time, too, he was contributing articles to the *Republican* of which he was now the nominal editor and which he helped to print. Like most journals of its kind it had a short life, failing in 1888 shortly after his mother began her monthly paper,

The Dawn, under the pseudonym of 'Dora Falconer'. By now an ardent suffragette and fighter for women's rights, a role she was to play almost until her death in 1922, her paper was printed, published and managed almost entirely by women, except for one male who had had some printing experience. *The Dawn* existed for longer than seventeen years, closing down in 1905.

Established as a poet, Lawson was slow to turn to fiction and his first story, 'His Father's Mate' was not published until 22 December 1888. A few days later his father, who had proudly shown his son's story in the *Bulletin* to his friends, died at Mount Victoria. One of Lawson's props had given way for it is evident from the visits he made to his father, whose building contracts were now centred in the Blue Mountains, that there was a strong bond between the two men — one that Louisa had deliberately tried to break when she took Henry to live with her in Sydney. He was to admit that there were faults on both sides in the break-up of his parents' marriage but his emotionally charged story 'A Child in the Dark and a Foreign Father' would not have pleased his mother.

Measured in terms of income, the life of the freelance writer in the 1890s who sought to live by writing alone, was even more precarious than it is today. Lawson, despite his increasing popularity, was still eking out a penurious livelihood by working at his trade whenever work was available.

Bent on a journalistic career, he travelled to Western Australia where he found conditions no better than they were at Sydney. He did contribute a series of articles to the newly founded *Albany Observer*. A few months later, in 1891, he joined the short-lived Brisbane *Boomerang*, edited by Gresley Lukin, as a columnist, and was a staff writer for six months at a wage of £2 per week.

Insecure, dejected, and frustrated, already addicted to alcohol, Lawson never ceased to believe in his own ability as a writer and by 1892, the year in which Archibald sent him to the town of Bourke 500 miles from Sydney to report on the great drought of 1892-93, he was seriously mastering the short story. Bourke provided him with an insight into the unionism of the nomadic shearers and bush workers and their creed of mateship which he was to make an article of faith for Australia.

Still desperate, still drinking, but still a fervent radical, an attitude which undoubtedly limited his opportunities for employment, if nothing else did, in 1894 he helped his mother produce his first book, '*Short Stories in Prose and Verse*', at the office of the *Dawn*. It was favourably received despite an introduction deploring local and overseas attitudes to Australian writing, but at a retail price of 1/- it brought no financial return.

Well known and well liked in literary circles, friendly with Mary Gilmore, Victor Daley, E. J. Brady, Roderic Quinn and Le Gay Brereton, read, quoted and discussed wherever the *Bulletin*, the *Worker*, or John Norton's Sydney *Truth* were circulating, with a book of poems, '*In the Days When the World was Wide*' in print and '*While the Billy Boils*', a book of short stories, in the press, both from the already prestigious publishers, Angus & Robertson, Lawson was at the height of his powers. Both books consolidated his place in the affections of the Australian public.

In the midst of this personal excitement Lawson married Bertha Bredt, who had met him the year previously whilst on a visit to her mother, now married to William McNamara, a leading radical bookseller in Sydney, and like Lawson's mother, destined to carve out a career for herself and later to be known as The Mother of the Labor Party. Another of her daughters, Hilda, had married in 1895 John Thomas Lang, a future Premier of New South Wales.

The marriage of Henry and Bertha proved as unhappy as their mutual friends had warned it would. To get Henry away from temptation she had gone with him on desperate trips to Western Australia and New Zealand, where his son, James, was born in March 1898. Bland Holt, a generous actor-manager, had commissioned and paid Henry for a drama which proved unplayable, but the money thus earned provided them with the means to return to Sydney in April. Between drinking bouts Lawson continued to write but by the end of the year he was for a time in a clinic for inebriates — nor was it to be the only time.

Lawson was still in his early thirties when he sailed for London, the Mecca of all successful colonial authors, in April 1900, accompanied by his wife and two children, his daughter Bertha a month old. Armed with the inevitable letters of introduction to editors and agents, his expenses paid by friends and supporters, he would begin a new life.

For a time his high hopes, and those of his friends seemed justified. J. B. Pinker, London's leading literary agent, was managing his affairs, he had received encouragement from English critics and his stories were being published in leading periodicals. But loneliness and the climate told in the end and he began drinking heavily again. Bertha's health gave way under the strain and by the end of 1902 they were back in Sydney from what Lawson wrote later was 'the run to England that almost ruined me'. It did.

The bitter years were about to begin. His wife in 1903 obtained a judicial separation and failure to comply with a maintenance order resulted in Henry spending various terms, over a period of years, in Long Bay gaol.

His literary powers declined with a general breakdown in health and only occasionally did flashes of his former genius appear to delight his readers.

He came to rely as much on the bounty of his friends as he did on the small literary pension paid by the Federal Government on his behalf to his 'little landlady, Mrs Byers', at whose small cottage in Abbotsford he died on 2 September 1922.

Given a State funeral and buried in Waverley Cemetery, he was remembered on all sides as 'The People's Poet'. He would have liked that.

WALTER STONE

11

The Teams

A CLOUD of dust on the long, white road,
   And the teams go creeping on
Inch by inch with the weary load;
And by the power of the green-hide goad
   The distant goal is won.

With eyes half-shut to the blinding dust,
   And necks to the yokes bent low,
The beasts are pulling as bullocks must;
And the shining tires might almost rust
   While the spokes are turning slow.

With face half-hid by a broad-brimmed hat,
   That shades from the heat's white waves,
And shouldered whip, with its green-hide plait,
The driver plods with a gait like that
   Of his weary, patient slaves.

He wipes his brow, for the day is hot,
   And spits to the left with spite;
He shouts at Bally, and flicks at Scot,
And raises dust from the back of Spot,
   And spits to the dusty right.

He'll sometimes pause as a thing of form
   In front of a settler's door,
And ask for a drink, and remark "It's warm".
Or say "There's signs of a thunderstorm";
   But he seldom utters more.

The rains are heavy on roads like these
   And, fronting his lonely home,
For days together the settler sees
The waggons bogged to the axletrees,
   Or ploughing the sodden loam.

And then, when the roads are at their worst,
   The bushman's children hear
The cruel blows of the whips reversed
While bullocks pull as their hearts would burst,
   And bellow with pain and fear.

And thus—with glimpses of home and rest—
   Are the long, long journeys done;
And thus—'tis a thankless life at the best!—
Is Distance fought in the mighty West,
   And the lonely battle won.

THE TEAMS
Oil on hardboard 14 in. × 18 in. 1973

The Shearer's Dream

Oh, I dreamt I shore in a shearin'-shed, and it was a dream of joy,
For every one of the rouseabouts was a girl dressed up as a boy—
Dressed up like a page in a pantomime, and the prettiest ever seen—
They had flaxen hair, they had coal-black hair—and every shade
    between.

There was short, plump girls, there was tall, slim girls, and the
    handsomest ever seen—
They was four-foot-five, they was six-foot high, and every height
    between.

The shed was cooled by electric fans that was over every shoot;
The pens was of polished ma-ho-gany, and everything else to suit;
The huts had springs to the mattresses, and the tucker was simply
    grand,
And every night by the billerbong we danced to a German band.

Our pay was the wool on the jumbucks' backs, so we shore till all
    was blue—
The sheep was washed afore they was shore (and the rams was
    scented too);
And we all of us wept when the shed cut out, in spite of the long,
    hot days,
For every hour them girls waltzed in with whisky and beer on
    tr-a-a-ays!

There was three of them girls to every chap, and as jealous as they
    could be—
There was three of them girls to every chap, and six of 'em picked
    on me;
We was draftin' them out for the homeward track and sharin' 'em
    round like steam,
When I woke with me head in the blazin' sun to find 'twas a
    shearer's dream.

14

THE SHEARER'S DREAM
Oil on hardboard 14 in. × 18 in. 1973

Jack Dunn of Nevertire

IT chanced upon the very day we'd got the shearing done,
A buggy brought a stranger to the West-o'-Sunday Run;
He had a round and jolly face, and sleek he was and stout—
He drove right up between the huts and called the super out.
We chaps were smoking after tea, and heard the swell inquire
For one as travelled by the name of "Dunn of Nevertire".
>   Jack Dunn of Nevertire,
>   Old Dunn of Nevertire;
> There wasn't one of us but knew Jack Dunn of Nevertire.

"Jack Dunn of Nevertire," he said; "I was a mate of his;
And now it's twenty years since I set eyes upon his phiz.
There is no whiter man than Jack—no straighter south the line,
There is no hand in all the land I'd sooner grip in mine;
To help a mate in trouble Jack would go through flood and fire.
Great Scott! and don't you know the name of Dunn of Nevertire?
>   Big Dunn of Nevertire,
>   Long Jack from Nevertire;
> He stuck to me through thick and thin, Jack Dunn of Nevertire.

"I did a wild and foolish thing while Jack and I were mates,
And I disgraced my guv'nor's name, an' wished to try the States.
My lamps were turned to Yankee-land, for I'd some people there.
And I was 'right' when someone sent the money for my fare;
I thought 'twas Dad, until I took the trouble to inquire
And found the man who sent the stuff was Dunn of Nevertire,
>   Jack Dunn of Nevertire,
>   Soft Dunn of Nevertire;
> He'd won some money on a race—Jack Dunn of Nevertire.

"Now I've returned, by Liverpool, a swell of Yankee brand;
I reckon, guess, and kalkilate to wake my native land;
There is no better land, I swear, in all the wide world round—
I smelt the bush a month before we touched King George's Sound
And now I've come to settle down, the top of my desire
Is just to meet a mate o' mine called 'Dunn of Nevertire'.
>   Was raised at Nevertire—
>   The town of Nevertire;
> He humped his bluey by the name of 'Dunn of Nevertire'.

"I've heard he's poor, and if he is, a proud old fool is he;
But, spite of that, I'll find a way to fix the old gumtree.
I've bought a station in the North—the best that could be had;
I want a man to pick the stock—I want a super bad;
I want no bully-brute to boss—no crawling, sneaking liar—
My station super's name shall be 'Jack Dunn of Nevertire!"
>   Straight Dunn of Nevertire,
>   Proud Jack from Nevertire;
> I guess he's known up Queensland way—Jack Dunn of Nevertire."

JACK DUNN OF NEVERTIRE
Oil on hardboard 18 in. × 14 in. 1973

The super said, while to his face a strange expression came:
"I *think* I've seen the man you want, I *think* I know the name;
Had he a jolly kind of face, a free and careless way,
Grey eyes that always seemed to smile, and hair just turning grey—
Clean-shaved, except a light moustache, long-limbed, an' tough as
            wire?"
"THAT'S HIM! THAT'S DUNN!" the stranger roared, "Jack Dunn of
      Nevertire!"
                  John Dunn of Nevertire,
                  Jack D. from Nevertire,
They said I'd find him here, the cuss!—Jack Dunn of Nevertire.

"I'd know his walk," the stranger cried, "though sobered, I'll allow."
"I doubt it much," the boss replied, "he don't walk that way now."
"Perhaps he don't!" the stranger said, "if years were hard on Jack;
But, if he were a mile away, I swear I'd know his back."
"I doubt it much," the super said, and sadly puffed his briar,
"I guess he wears a pair of wings—Jack Dunn of Nevertire;
                  Jack Dunn of Nevertire,
                  Brave Dunn of Nevertire,
He caught a fever nursing me, Jack Dunn of Nevertire."

We took the stranger round to where a gum-tree stood alone,
And in the grass beside the trunk he saw a granite stone;
The names of Dunn and Nevertire were plainly written there—
"I'm all broke up," the stranger said, in sorrow and despair,
"I guess he has a wider run, the man that I require;
He's got a river-frontage now, Jack Dunn of Nevertire;
                  Straight Dunn of Nevertire,
                  White Jack from Nevertire,
I guess Saint Peter knew the name of 'Dunn of Nevertire'."

Eureka
(A Fragment)

ROLL up, Eureka's heroes, on that Grand Old Rush afar,
For Lalor's gone to join you in the big camp where you are;
Roll up and give him welcome such as only diggers can,
For well he battled for the rights of miner and of Man.
In that bright, golden country that lies beyond our sight,
The record of his honest life shall be his Miner's Right;
But many a bearded mouth shall twitch, and many a tear be shed,
And many a grey old digger sigh to hear that Lalor's dead.
Yet wipe your eyes, old fossikers, o'er worked-out fields that roam,
You need not weep at parting from a digger going home.

Now from the strange wild seasons past, the days of golden strife,
Now from the Roaring Fifties comes a scene from Lalor's life:
All gleaming white amid the shafts o'er gully, hill, and flat
Again I see the tents that form the camp at Ballarat.
I hear the shovels and the picks, and all the air is rife
With the rattle of the cradles and the sounds of digger-life;
The clatter of the windlass-boles, as spinning round they go,
And then the signal to his mate, the digger's cry, "Below!"
From many a busy pointing-forge the sound of labour swells,
The tinkling at the anvils is as clear as silver bells.
I hear the broken English from the mouth of many a one
From every state and nation that is known beneath the sun;
The homely tongue of Scotland and the brogue of Ireland blend
With the dialects of England, right from Berwick to Land's End;
And to the busy concourse here the States have sent a part,
The land of gulches that has been immortalized by Harte;
The land where long from mining-camps the blue smoke upward
    curled;
The land that gave the "Partner" true and "Mliss" unto the world;
The men from all the nations in the New World and the Old,
All side by side, like brethren here, are delving after gold.
But suddenly the warning cries are heard on every side
As, closing in around the field, a ring of troopers ride.
Unlicensed diggers are the game—their class and want are sins,
And so, with all its shameful scenes, the digger-hunt begins.
The men are seized who are too poor the heavy tax to pay,
Chained man to man as convicts were, and dragged in gangs away.
Though in the eye of many a man the menace scarce was hid,
The diggers' blood was slow to boil, but scalded when it did.

But now another match is lit that soon must fire the charge,
A digger murdered in the camp; his murderer at large!
"Roll up! Roll up!" the poignant cry awakes the evening air,
And angry faces surge like waves around the speakers there.
"What are our sins that we should be an outlawed class?" they say,
"Shall we stand by while mates are seized and dragged like lags away?
Shall insult be on insult heaped? Shall we let these things go?"

19

And with a roar of voices comes the diggers' answer—"No!"
The day has vanished from the scene, but not the air of night
Can cool the blood that, ebbing back, leaves brows in anger white.
Lo, from the roof of Bentley's inn the flames are leaping high;
They write "Revenge!" in letters red across the smoke-dimmed sky.
"To arms! To arms!" the cry is out; "To arms and play your part;
For every pike upon a pole will find a tyrant's heart!"
Now Lalor comes to take the lead, the spirit does not lag,
And down the rough, wild diggers kneel beneath the Diggers' Flag;
Then, rising to their feet, they swear, while rugged hearts beat high,
To stand beside their leader and to conquer or to die!
Around Eureka's stockade now the shades of night close fast,
Three hundred sleep beside their arms, and thirty sleep their last.

About the streets of Melbourne town the sound of bells is borne
That call the citizens to prayer that fateful Sabbath morn;
But there, upon Eureka's hill, a hundred miles away,
The diggers' forms lie white and still above the blood-stained clay.
The bells that toll the diggers' death might also ring a knell
For those few gallant soldiers, dead, who did their duty well.
The sight of murdered heroes is to hero-hearts a goad,
A thousand men are up in arms upon the Creswick road,
And wildest rumours in the air are flying up and down,
'Tis said the men of Ballarat will march on Melbourne town.
But not in vain those diggers died. Their comrades may rejoice,
For o'er the voice of tyranny is heard the people's voice;
It says: "Reform your rotten law, the diggers' wrongs make right,
Or else with them, our brothers now, we'll gather to the fight."

'Twas of such stuff the men were made who saw our nation born,
And such as Lalor were the men who led the vanguard on;
And like such men may we be found, with leaders such as they,
In the roll-up of Australians on our darkest, grandest day!

EUREKA
Oil on hardboard 18 in. × 14 in. 1973

The Wander-Light

Oh, my ways are strange ways and new ways and old ways,
And deep ways and steep ways and high ways and low;
I'm at home and at ease on a track that I know not
And restless and lost on a road that I know.

Then they heard the tent-poles clatter,
  And the fly in twain was torn—
'Twas the soiled rag of a tatter
  Of the tent where I was born.
Does it matter? Which is stranger—
  Brick or stone or calico?—
There was One born in a manger
  Nineteen hundred years ago.

For my beds were camp beds and tramp beds and damp beds,
And my beds were dry beds on drought-stricken ground,
Hard beds and soft beds, and wide beds and narrow—
For my beds were strange beds the wide world round.

And the old hag seemed to ponder
  With her grey head nodding slow—
"He will dream, and he will wander
  Where but few would think to go.
He will flee the haunts of tailors,
  He will cross the ocean wide,
For his fathers they were sailors—
  All on his good father's side."

I rest not, 'tis best not, the world is a wide one—
And, caged for a moment, I pace to and fro;
I see things and dree things and plan while I'm sleeping,
I wander for ever and dream as I go.

And the old hag she was troubled
  As she bent above the bed;
"He will dream things and he'll see things
  To come true when he is dead.
He will see things all too plainly,
  And his fellows will deride,
For his mothers they were gipsies—
  All on his good mother's side."

And my dreams are strange dreams, are day dreams, are grey dreams,
And my dreams are wild dreams, and old dreams and new;
They haunt me and daunt me with fears of the morrow—
My brothers they doubt me—but my dreams come true.

THE WANDER-LIGHT
Oil on hardboard 14 in. × 10 in. 1973

The Shearing-Shed

"THE ladies are coming," the super says
    To the shearers sweltering there,
And "the ladies" means in the shearing-shed:
    "Don't cut 'em too bad. Don't swear."
The ghost of a pause in the shed's rough heart,
    And lower is bowed each head;
Then nothing is heard save a whispered word
    And the roar of the shearing-shed.

The tall, shy rouser has lost his wits;
    His limbs are all astray;
He leaves a fleece on the shearing-board
    And his broom in the shearer's way.
There's a curse in store for that jackeroo
    As down by the wall he slants—
But the ringer bends with his legs askew
    And wishes he'd "patched them pants".

They are girls from the city. Our hearts rebel
    As we squint at their dainty feet,
While they gush and say in a girly way
    That "the dear little lambs" are "sweet".
And Bill the Ringer, who'd scorn the use
    Of a childish word like damn,
Would give a pound that his tongue were loose
    As he tackles a lively lamb.

Swift thought of home in the coastal towns—
    Or rivers and waving grass—
And a weight on our hearts that we cannot define
    That comes as the ladies pass;
But the rouser ventures a nervous dig
    With his thumb in the next man's back;
And Bogan says to his pen-mate: "Twig
    The style of that last un, Jack."

Jack Moonlight gives her a careless glance—
    Then catches his breath with pain;
His strong hand shakes, and the sunbeams dance
    As he bends to his work again.
But he's well disguised in a bristling beard,
    Bronzed skin, and his shearer's dress;
And whatever he knew or hoped or feared
    Was hard for his mates to guess.

THE SHEARING-SHED
Oil on hardboard 14 in. × 18 in. 1973

Jack Moonlight, wiping his broad, white brow,
  Explains, with a doleful smile,
"A stitch in the side," and "I'm all right now"—
  But he leans on the beam awhile,
And gazes out in the blazing noon
  On the clearing, brown and bare . . . .
She had come and gone—like a breath of June
  In December's heat and glare.

Trooper Campbell

ONE day old Trooper Campbell
  Rode out to Blackman's Run;
His cap-peak and his sabre
  Were glancing in the sun.
'Twas New Year's Eve, and slowly
  Across the ridges low
The sad Old Year was drifting
  To where the old years go.

The trooper's mind was reading
  The love-page of his life—
His love for Mary Wylie
  Ere she was Blackman's wife;
He sorrowed for the sorrows
  Of the heart a rival won,
For he knew that there was trouble
  Out there on Blackman's Run.

The sapling shades had lengthened,
  The summer day was late,
When Blackman met the trooper
  Beyond the homestead gate;
And, if the hand of trouble
  Can leave a lasting trace,
The lines of care had come to stay
  On poor old Blackman's face.

"Not good day, Trooper Campbell,
  It's a bad, bad day for me—
You are of all the men on earth
  The one I wished to see.
The great black clouds of trouble
  Above our homestead hang;
That wild and reckless boy of mine
  Has joined M'Durmer's gang.

"Oh! save him, save him, Campbell,
  I beg in friendship's name!
For if they take and hang him,
  The wife would die of shame.
Could Mary and her sisters
  Hold up their heads again,
And face a woman's malice,
  Or claim the love of men?

"And if he does a murder
  We all were better dead.
Don't take him living, Trooper,
  If a price be on his head;
But shoot him! shoot him, Campbell,

When you meet him face to face,
And save him from the gallows—
And us from that disgrace.''

"Now, Tom,'' cried Trooper Campbell,
"You know your words are wild.
Wild though he is and reckless,
Yet still he is your child;
Bear up and face your trouble,
Yes, meet it like a man,
And tell the wife and daughters
I'll save him if I can.''

The sad Australian sunset
Had faded from the west;
But night brought darker shadows
To hearts that could not rest;
And Blackman's wife sat rocking
And moaning in her chair.
"Oh, the disgrace, disgrace,'' she moaned;
"It's more than I can bear.

"In hardship and in trouble
I struggled year by year
To make my children better
Than other children here.
And if my son's a felon
How can I show my face?
I cannot bear disgrace; my God,
I cannot bear disgrace!

"Ah, God in Heaven pardon!
I'm selfish in my woe—
My boy is better-hearted
Than many that I know.
I'll face whatever happens,
And, till his mother's dead,
My foolish child shall find a place
To lay his outlawed head.''

Sore-hearted, Trooper Campbell
Rode out from Blackman's Run,
Nor noticed aught about him
Till thirteen miles were done;
When, close beside a cutting,
He heard the click of locks,
And saw the rifle-muzzles
Trained on him from the rocks.

TROOPER CAMPBELL
Oil on hardboard 14 in. × 18 in. 1973

But suddenly a youth rode out,
    And, close by Campbell's side:
"Don't fire! don't fire, in Heaven's name!
    It's Campbell, boys!" he cried.
Then one by one in silence
    The levelled rifles fell,
For who'd shoot Trooper Campbell
    Of those who knew him well?

On, bravely sat old Campbell,
    No sign of fear showed he.
He slowly drew his carbine;
    It rested by his knee.
The outlaws' guns were lifted,
    But none the silence broke,
Till steadfastly and firmly
    Old Trooper Campbell spoke,

"The boy that you would ruin
    Goes home with me, my men;
Or some of us shall never
    Ride through the Gap again.
You all know Trooper Campbell,
    And have you ever heard
That bluff or lead could turn him
    Or make him break his word?

"That reckless lad is playing
    A heartless villain's part;
He knows that he is breaking
    His poor old mother's heart.
He's going straight to ruin;
    But 'tis not that alone,
He'll bring dishonour to a name
    That I'd be proud to own.

"I speak to you, M'Durmer—
    If your heart's not granite quite,
And if you'd seen the trouble
    At Blackman's home tonight,
You'd help me now, M'Durmer—
    I speak as man to man—
I swore to save the foolish lad—
    I'll save him if I can."

"Oh, take him!" said M'Durmer,
    He's got a horse to ride . . . ."
The youngster thought a moment,
    Then rode to Campbell's side . . . .
"Good-bye!" young Blackman shouted,

As up the range they sped.
"Luck for the New Year, Campbell,"
    Was all M'Durmer said.

Then fast along the ridges
    Two horsemen rode a race,
The moonlight lent a glory
    To Trooper Campbell's face.
And ere the new year's dawning
    They reached the homestead gate—
"I found him," said the Trooper,
    "And not, thank God, too late!"

The Sliprails and the Spur

THE colours of the setting sun
    Withdrew across the Western land—
He raised the sliprails, one by one,
    And shot them home with trembling hand;
Her brown hands clung—her face grew pale—
    Ah! quivering chin and eyes that brim!—
One quick, fierce kiss across the rail,
    And, "Good-bye, Mary!" "Good-bye, Jim!"

Oh, he rides hard to race the pain
    Who rides from love, who rides from home;
But he rides slowly home again,
    Whose heart has learnt to love and roam.

A hand upon the horse's mane,
    And one foot in the stirrup set,
And, stooping back to kiss again,
    With "Good-bye, Mary! don't you fret!
When I come back"—he laughed for her—
    "We do not know how soon 'twill be;
I'll whistle as I round the spur—
    You let the sliprails down for me."

She gasped for sudden loss of hope,
    As, with a backward wave to her,
He cantered down the grassy slope
    And swiftly round the darkening spur.
Black-pencilled panels standing high,
    And darkness fading into stars,
And, blurring fast against the sky,
    A faint white form beside the bars.

And often at the set of sun,
    In winter bleak and summer brown,
She'd steal across the little run,
    And shyly let the sliprails down,
And listen there when darkness shut
    The nearer spur in silence deep,
And when they called her from the hut
    Steal home and cry herself to sleep.

And he rides hard to dull the pain
    Who rides from one that loves him best . . .
And he rides slowly back again,
    Whose restless heart must rove for rest.

THE SLIPRAILS AND THE SPUR
Oil on hardboard 18 in. × 14 in. 1973

The Lights of Cobb and Co.

FIRE lighted; on the table a meal for sleepy men;
A lantern in the stable; a jingle now and then;
The mail-coach looming darkly by light of moon and star;
The growl of sleepy voices; a candle in the bar;
A stumble in the passage of folk with wits abroad;
A swear-word from a bedroom—the shout of "All aboard!"
"Tchk tchk! Git-up!" "Hold fast, there!" and down the range we go;
Five hundred miles of scattered camps will watch for Cobb and Co.

Old coaching towns already decaying for their sins;
Uncounted "Half-Way Houses", and scores of "Ten-Mile Inns";
The riders from the stations by lonely granite peaks;
The black-boy for the shepherds on sheep and cattle creeks;
The roaring camps of Gulgong, and many a "Digger's Rest";
The diggers on the Lachlan; the huts of Farthest West;
Some twenty thousand exiles who sailed for weal or woe—
The bravest hearts of twenty lands will wait for Cobb and Co.

The morning star has vanished, the frost and fog are gone,
In one of those grand mornings which but on mountains dawn;
A flask of friendly whisky—each other's hopes we share—
And throw our top-coats open to drink the mountain air.
The roads are rare to travel, and life seems all complete;
The grind of wheels on gravel, the trot of horses' feet,
The trot, trot, trot and canter, as down the spur we go—
The green sweeps to horizons blue that call for Cobb and Co.

We take a bright girl actress through western dusts and damps,
To bear the home-world message, and sing for sinful camps,
To stir our hearts and break them, wild hearts that hope and ache—
(Ah! when she thinks again of these her own must nearly break!)
Five miles this side the gold-field, a loud, triumphant shout:
Five hundred cheering diggers have snatched the horses out:
With "Auld Lang Syne" in chorus, through roaring camps they go
That cheer for her, and cheer for Home, and cheer for Cobb and Co.

Three lamps above the ridges and gorges dark and deep,
A flash on sandstone cuttings where sheer the sidlings sweep,
A flash on shrouded waggons, on water ghastly white;
Weird bush and scattered remnants of "rushes in the night";
Across the swollen river a flash beyond the ford:
Ride hard to warn the driver! He's drunk or mad, good Lord!
But on the bank to westward a broad and cheerful glow—
New camps extend across the plains new routes for Cobb and Co.

THE LIGHTS OF COBB AND CO.
Oil on hardboard 16 in. × 20 in. 1973

Swift scramble up the sidling where teams climb inch by inch;
Pause, bird-like, on the summit—then breakneck down the pinch;
By clear, ridge-country rivers, and gaps where tracks run high,
Where waits the lonely horseman, cut clear against the sky;
Past haunted half-way houses—where convicts made the bricks—
Scrub-yards and new bark shanties, we dash with five and six;
Through stringy-bark and blue-gum, and box and pine we go—
A hundred miles shall see tonight the lights of Cobb and Co.!

Song of Old Joe Swallow

WHEN I was up the country in the rough and early days,
I used to work along of Jimmy Nowlett's bullick-drays;
Then the reelroad wasn't heered on, an' the bush was wild an' strange,
An' we useter draw the timber from the saw-pits in the range—
Load provisions for the stations, an' we'd travel far and slow
Through the plains an' 'cross the ranges in the days of long ago.

Then it's yoke up the bullicks and tramp beside 'em slow,
An' saddle up yer horses an' a-ridin' we well go,
To the bullick-drivin', cattle-drovin'
Nigger, digger, roarin', rovin'
Days o' long ago.

Once me an Jimmy Nowlett loaded timber for the town,
But we hadn't gone a dozen mile before the rain come down,
An' me an' Jimmy Nowlett an' the bullicks an' the dray
Was cut off on some risin' ground while floods around us lay;
An' we soon run short of tucker an' terbaccer, which was bad,
An' pertaters dipped in honey was the only tuck we had.

Then half our bullicks perished, when a drought was on the land,
In the burnin' heat that dazzles as it dances on the sand;
But in spite of barren ridges, an' in spite of mud, an' heat,
An' the dust that browned the bushes when it rose from bullicks' feet,
An' in spite of modern progress, and in spite of all their blow,
'Twas a better land to live in, in the days o' long ago.

When the frosty moon was shinin' o'er the ranges like a lamp,
An' a lot of bullick-drivers was a-campin' on the camp,
When the fire was blazin' cheery an' the pipes was drawin' well,
Then our songs we useter chorus an' our yarns we useter tell;
An' we'd talk of lands we come from, and of chaps we useter know,
For there always was behind us other days o' long ago.

Ah, them early days was ended when the reelroad crossed the plain,
But in dreams I often tramp beside the bullick-team again:
Still we pauses at the shanty just to have a drop o' cheer,
Still I feels a kind of pleasure when the campin'-ground is near;
Still I smells the old tarpaulin me an Jimmy useter throw
'Cross the timber-track for shelter in the days of long ago.

I have been a-drifting back'ards with the changes of the land,
An' if I spoke to bullicks now they wouldn't understand;
But when Mary wakes me sudden in the night I'll often say:
"Come here, Spot, an' stan' up, Bally, blank an' blank an' come-
    eer-way."
An' she says that, when I'm sleepin', oft my elerquince 'ill flow
In the bullick-drivin' language of the days o' long ago.

Well, the pub will soon be closin', so I'll give the thing a rest;
But if you should drop on Nowlett in the far an' distant west—
An' if Jimmy uses doubleyou instead of ar or vee,
An' if he drops his aitches, then you're sure to know it's he.
An' you won't forgit to arsk him if he still remembers Joe.
As knowed him up the country in the days o' long ago.

*Then it's yoke up the bullicks and tramp beside
        em slow,*
An' saddle up yer horses an' a-ridin' we will go,
To the bullick-drivin', cattle-drovin'
Nigger, digger, roarin', rovin'
Days o' long ago.

SONG OF OLD JOE SWALLOW
Oil on hardboard 14 in. × 18 in. 1973

Andy's Gone With Cattle

OUR Andy's gone with cattle now—
  Our hearts are out of order—
With drought he's gone to battle now
  Across the Queensland border.

He's left us in dejection now;
  Our thoughts with him are roving;
It's dull on this selection now,
  Since Andy went a-droving.

Who now shall wear the cheerful face
  In times when things are slackest?
And who shall whistle round the place
  When Fortune frowns her blackest?

Oh, who shall cheek the squatter now
  When he comes round us snarling?
His tongue is growing hotter now
  Since Andy crossed the Darling.

Oh, may the showers in torrents fall,
  And all the tanks run over;
And may the grass grow green and tall
  In pathways of the drover;

And may good angels send the rain
  On desert stretches sandy;
And when the summer comes again
  God grant 'twill bring us Andy.

ANDY'S GONE WITH CATTLE
Oil on hardboard 14 in. × 18 in. 1973

The Glass on the Bar

THREE bushmen one morning rode up to an inn,
And one of them call for the drinks with a grin;
They'd only returned from a trip to the North,
And, eager to greet them, the landlord came forth.
He absently poured out a glass of Three Star,
And set down that drink with the rest on the bar.

"There, that is for Harry," he said, "and it's queer,
'Tis the very same glass that he drank from last year;
His name's on the glass, you can read it like print,
He scratched it himself with an old bit of flint;
I remember his drink — it was always Three Star" —
And the landlord looked out through the door of the bar.

He looked at the horses, and counted but three:
"You were always together—where's Harry?" cried he.
Oh, sadly they looked at the glass as they said,
"You may put it away, for our old mate is dead;"
But one, gazing out o'er the ridges afar,
Said, "We owe him a shout—leave the glass on the bar."

They thought of the far-away grave on the plain,
They thought of the comrade who came not again,
They lifted their glasses, and sadly they said:
"We drink to the name of the mate who is dead."
And the sunlight streamed in, and a light like a star
Seemed to glow in the depth of the glass on the bar.

And still in that shanty a tumbler is seen,
It stands by the clock, always polished and clean;
And often the strangers will read as they pass
The name of a bushman engraved on the glass;
And though on the shelf but a dozen there are,
That glass never stands with the rest on the bar.

THE GLASS ON THE BAR
Oil on hardboard 14 in. × 18 in. 1973

The Cattle-Dog's Death

THE plains lay bare on the homeward route, .
And the march was heavy on man and brute;
For the Spirit of Drouth was on all the land,
And the white heat danced on the glowing sand.

The best of our cattle-dogs lagged at last;
His strength gave out ere the plains were passed;
And our hearts were sad as he crept and laid
His languid limbs in the nearest shade.

He saved our lives in the years gone by,
When no one dreamed of the danger nigh,
And treacherous blacks in the darkness crept
On the silent camp where the white men slept.

"Rover is dying," a stockman said,
As he knelt and lifted the shaggy head;
"'Tis a long day's march ere the run be near,
And he's going fast; shall we leave him here?"

But the super cried, "There's an answer there!"
As he raised a tuft of the dog's grey hair;
And, strangely vivid, each man descried
The old spear-mark on the shaggy hide.

We laid a bluey and coat across
A camp-pack strapped on the lightest horse,
Then raised the dog to his deathbed high,
And brought him far 'neath the burning sky.

At the kindly touch of the stockmen rude
His eyes grew human with gratitude;
And though we were parched, when his eyes grew dim
The last of our water was given to him.

The super's daughter we knew would chide
If we left the dog in the desert wide;
So we carried him home o'er the burning sand
For a parting stroke from her small white hand.

But long ere the station was seen ahead,
His pain was o'er, for Rover was dead;
And the folks all knew by our looks of gloom
'Twas a comrade's corpse that we carried home.

THE CATTLE-DOG'S DEATH
Oil on hardboard 14 in. × 18 in. 1973

Mary Called Him Mister

THEY'D parted just a year ago—she thought he'd ne'er come back;
She stammered, blushed, held out her hand, and called him "Mister
    Mack".
How could he know that all the while she longed to murmur "John"?—
He called her "Miss le Brook", and asked "How she was getting on".

They'd parted but a year before; they'd loved each other well,
But he'd been down to Sydney since, and come back *such* a swell.
They longed to meet in fond embrace, they hungered for a kiss —
But Mary called him *Mister*, and the idiot called her *Miss*.

He paused, and leaned against the door—a stupid chap was he—
And, when she asked if he'd come in and have a cup of tea,
He looked to left, he looked to right, and then he glanced behind . . .
And slowly doffed his cabbage-tree . . . and said he "didn't mind".

She made a shy apology because the meat was tough,
Then asked if he was quite, quite sure the tea was sweet enough;
He stirred his tea, and sipped it twice, and answered "plenty quite".
And cut himself a slice of beef, and said that it was "right".

She glanced at him, at times, and coughed an awkward little cough;
He stared at anything but her and said, "I must be off".
That evening he went riding north—a sad and lonely ride—
She locked herself inside her room, and sat her down and cried.

They'd parted but a year before, they loved each other well—
But she was *such* a country girl and he'd grown such a swell;
They longed to meet in fond embrace, they hungered for a kiss—
But Mary called him *Mister*, and the idiot called her *Miss*.

MARY CALLED HIM MISTER
Oil on hardboard 14 in. × 18 in. 1973

Song of the Old Bullock-Driver

FAR back in the days when the blacks used to ramble
  In long single file 'neath the evergreen tree,
The wool-teams in season came down from Coonamble,
  And journeyed for weeks on their way to the sea.
'Twas then that our hearts and our sinews were stronger,
  For those were the days when tough bushmen were bred.
We journeyed on roads that were rougher and longer
  Than roads which the feet of our grandchildren tread.

We never were lonely, for, camping together,
  We yarned and we smoked the long evenings away,
And little I cared for the signs of the weather
  When snug in my hammock slung under the dray.
We rose with the dawn, were it ever so chilly,
  When yokes and tarpaulins were covered with frost,
And toasted the bacon and boiled the black billy—
  Then high on the camp-fire the branches we tossed.

On flats where the air was suggestive of possums,
  And homesteads and fences were hinting of change,
We saw the faint glimmer of apple-tree blossoms,
  And far in the distance the blue of the range;
Out there in the rain there was small use in flogging
  The poor tortured bullocks that tugged at the load,
When down to the axles, the waggons were bogging
  And traffic was making a slough of the road.

Oh, hard on the beasts were those terrible pinches
  Where two teams of bullocks were yoked to a load,
And tugging and slipping, and moving by inches,
  Half-way to the summit they clung to the road.
And then, when the last of the pinches was bested,
  (You'll surely not say that a glass was a sin?)
The bullocks lay down 'neath the gum-trees and rested—
  The bullockies steered for the door of the inn.

Then slowly we crawled by the trees that kept tally
  Of miles that were passed on the long journey down.
We saw the wild beauty of Capertee Valley,
  As slowly we rounded the base of the Crown.
But, ah! the poor bullocks were cruelly goaded
  While climbing the hills from the flats and the vales;
'Twas here that the teams were so often unloaded
  That all knew the meaning of "counting your bales".

SONG OF THE OLD BULLOCK-DRIVER
Oil on hardboard 14 in. × 18 in. 1973

The best-paying load that I ever have carried
    Was the one to the run where my sweetheart was nurse.
We courted awhile, and agreed to get married,
    And couple our futures for better or worse.
And when my old feet were too weary to drag on
    The miles of rough metal they met by the way,
My eldest grew up and I gave him the waggon—
    He's plodding along by the bullocks today.

Ballad of the Drover

ACROSS the stony ridges,
  Across the rolling plain,
Young Harry Dale, the drover,
  Comes riding home again.
And well his stock-horse bears him,
  And light of heart is he,
And stoutly his old packhorse
  Is trotting by his knee.

Up Queensland way with cattle
  He's travelled regions vast,
And many months have vanished
  Since home-folks saw him last.
He hums a song of someone
  He hopes to marry soon;
And hobble-chains and camp-ware
  Keep jingling to the tune.

Beyond the hazy dado
  Against the lower skies
And yon blue line of ranges
  The station homestead lies.
And thitherward the drover
  Jogs through the lazy noon,
While hobble-chains and camp-ware
  Are jingling to a tune.

An hour has filled the heavens
  With storm-clouds inky black;
At times the lightning trickles
  Around the drover's track;
But Harry pushes onward,
  His horses' strength he tries,
In hope to reach the river
  Before the flood shall rise.

The thunder, pealing o'er him,
  Goes rumbling down the plain;
And sweet on thirsty pastures
  Beats fast the plashing rain;
Then every creek and gully
  Sends forth its tribute flood—
The river runs a banker,
  All stained with yellow mud.

Now Harry speaks to Rover,
  The best dog on the plains,

And to his hardy horses,
    And strokes their shaggy manes:
"We've breasted bigger rivers
    When floods were at their height,
Nor shall this gutter stop us
    From getting home tonight!"

The thunder growls a warning
    The blue, forked lightnings gleam;
The drover turns his horses
    To swim the fatal stream.
But, oh! the flood runs stronger
    Than e'er it ran before;
The saddle-horse is failing,
    And only half-way o'er!

When flashes next the lightning,
    The flood's grey breast is blank;
A cattle-dog and packhorse
    Are struggling up the bank.
But in the lonely homestead
    The girl shall wait in vain—
He'll never pass the stations
    In charge of stock again.

The faithful dog a moment
    Lies panting on the bank,
Then plunges through the current
    To where his master sank.
And round and round in circles
    He fights with failing strength,
Till, gripped by wilder waters,
    He fails and sinks at length.

Across the flooded lowlands
    And slopes of sodden loam
The packhorse struggles bravely
    To take dumb tidings home;
And mud-stained, wet, and weary,
    He goes by rock and tree,
With clanging chains and tinware
    All sounding eerily.

BALLAD OF THE DROVER
Oil on hardboard 14 in. × 18 in. 1973

Sticking to Bill

THERE's a thing that sends a lump to my throat,
  And cuts my heart like a knife:
'Tis the woman who waits at the prison gate,
  When the woman is not his wife.
You may preach and pray till the dawn of day,
  Denounce or damn as you will,
But the soul of that woman will cleave for aye
  To the sin-stained soul of Bill.

She has no use for our sympathy
  And her face is hard as a stone—
A rag of a woman, at war with the world
  And fiercely fighting alone.
At the kindly touch of the janitor's hand
  The eyes of a wife would fill,
But Sal replies with a "Blast yer eyes!"—
  She is only stickin' to Bill.

In spite of herself there is help that comes—
  And it comes from a source well hid—
To buy the tucker and pay the rent
  Of a roost for herself and kid.
For the "talent" has sent round its thievish hat
  By one with a fist and a will,
For a quid or two just to see Sal through—
  For Sal is stickin' to Bill.

A furtive figure from Nowhere comes
  To Red Rock Lane by night,
And it softly raps at a dingy door
  While it scowls to left and right:
It jerks its arm in a half salute,
  By habit—against its will;
'Tis a fellow felon of Bill's, discharged,
  And it brings her a message from Bill.

There's a woman who comes to the gate alone
  (Bill's Gaol Delivery's near),
With a face a little less like a stone
  And a sign of a savage tear;
With a suit of clobber done up and darned—
  For William is leaving "The Hill",
And the tear is the first she ever has shed
  Since she's been stickin' to Bill.

STICKING TO BILL
Oil on hardboard 14 in. × 18 in. 1973

There's tucker at home, and a job to come
    And no one to wish him ill,
There's a bottle of beer, and a minded kid
    In a brand-new suit of drill.
There's an old-time mate who will steer him straight,
    And the sticks of furniture still—
He can take a spell for a month if he likes,
    And—she's done her best for Bill.

Faces in the Street

THEY lie, the men who tell us, for reasons of their own,
That want is here a stranger, and that misery's unknown;
For where the nearest suburb and the city proper meet
My window-sill is level with the faces in the street—
    Drifting past, drifting past,
    To the beat of weary feet—
While I sorrow for the owners of those faces in the street.

And cause I have to sorrow, in a land so young and fair,
To see upon those faces stamped the marks of Want and Care;
I look in vain for traces of the fresh and fair and sweet
In sallow, sunken faces that are drifting through the street—
    Drifting on, drifting on,
    To the scrape of restless feet;
I can sorrow for the owners of the faces in the street.

In hours before the dawning dims the starlight in the sky
The wan and weary faces first begin to trickle by,
Increasing as the moments hurry on with morning feet,
Till like a pallid river flow the faces in the street—
    Flowing in, flowing in,
    To the beat of hurried feet—
Ah! I sorrow for the owners of those faces in the street.

The human river dwindles when 'tis past the hour of eight,
Its waves go flowing faster in the fear of being late;
But slowly drag the moments, whilst beneath the dust and heat
The city grinds the owners of the faces in the street—
    Grinding body, grinding soul,
    Yielding scarce enough to eat—
Oh! I sorrow for the owners of the faces in the street.

And then the only faces till the sun is sinking down
Are those of outside toilers and the idlers of the town,
Save here and there a face that seems a stranger in the street
Tells of the city's unemployed upon their weary beat—
    Drifting round, drifting round,
    To the tread of listless feet—
Ah! my heart aches for the owner of that sad face in the street.

And when the hours on lagging feet have slowly dragged away,
And sickly yellow gaslights rise to mock the going day,
Then, flowing past my window, like a tide in its retreat,
Again I see the pallid stream of faces in the street—
    Ebbing out, ebbing out,
    To the drag of tired feet,
While my heart is aching dumbly for the faces in the street.

And now all blurred and smirched with vice the day's sad end is seen,
For where the short "large hours" against the longer "small hours" lean,
With smiles that mock the wearer, and with words that half entreat,
Delilah pleads for custom at the corner of the street—
    Sinking down, sinking down,
    Battered wreck by tempests beat—
A dreadful, thankless trade is hers, that Woman of the Street.

But, ah! to dreader things than these our fair young city comes,
For in its heart are growing thick the filthy dens and slums,
Where human forms shall rot away in sties for swine unmeet
And ghostly faces shall be seen unfit for any street—
    Rotting out, rotting out,
    For the lack of air and meat—
In dens of vice and horror that are hidden from the street.

I wonder would the apathy of the wealthy men endure
Were all their windows level with the faces of the Poor?
Ah! Mammon's slaves, your knees shall knock, your hearts in terror beat,
When God demands a reason for the sorrows of the street,
    The wrong things and the bad things
    And the sad things that we meet
In the filthy lane and alley, and the cruel, heartless street.

I left the dreadful corner where the steps are never still,
And sought another window overlooking gorge and hill;
But when the night came dreary with the driving rain and sleet,
They haunted me—the shadows of those faces in the street,
    Flitting by, flitting by,
    Flitting by with noiseless feet,
And with cheeks that scarce were paler than the real ones in the street.

Once I cried: "O God Almighty! if Thy might doth still endure,
Now show me in a vision for the wrongs of Earth a cure."
And, lo, with shops all shuttered I beheld a city's street,
And in the warning distance heard the tramp of many feet,
    Coming near, coming near,
    To a drum's dull distant beat—
'Twas Despair's conscripted army that was marching down the street!

Then, like a swollen river that has broken bank and wall,
The human flood came pouring with the red flags over all,
And kindled eyes all blazing bright with revolution's heat,
And flashing swords reflecting rigid faces in the street—
    Pouring on, pouring on,
    To a drum's loud threatening beat,
And the war-hymns and the cheering of the people in the street.

FACES IN THE STREET
Oil on hardboard 14 in. × 18 in. 1973

And so it must be while the world goes rolling round its course,
The warning pen shall write in vain, the warning voice grow hoarse,
For not until a city feels Red Revolution's feet
Shall its sad people miss awhile the terrors of the street—
    The dreadful, everlasting strife
    For scarcely clothes and meat
In that pent track of living death—the city's cruel street.

Reedy River

TEN miles down Reedy River
   A pool of water lies,
And all the year it mirrors
   The changes in the skies.
Within that pool's broad bosom
   Is room for all the stars;
Its bed of sand has drifted
   O'er countless rocky bars.

Around the lower edges
   There waves a bed of reeds,
Where water-rats are hidden
   And where the wild-duck breeds;
And grassy slopes rise gently
   To ridges long and low,
Where groves of wattle flourish
   And native bluebells grow.

Beneath the granite ridges
   The eye may just discern
Where Rocky Creek emerges
   From deep green banks of fern;
And standing tall between them,
   The drooping sheoaks cool
The hard, blue-tinted waters
   Before they reach the pool.

Ten miles down Reedy River
   One Sunday afternoon,
I rode with Mary Campbell
   To that broad, bright lagoon;
We left our horses grazing
   Till shadows climbed the peak,
And strolled beneath the sheoaks
   On the banks of Rocky Creek.

Then home along the river
   That night we rode a race,
And the moonlight lent a glory
   To Mary Campbell's face;
I pleaded for my future
   All through that moonlight ride,
Until our weary horses
   Drew closer side by side.

Ten miles from Ryan's Crossing
   And five below the peak,

I built a little homestead
    On the banks of Rocky Creek;
I cleared the land and fenced it
    And ploughed the rich red loam;
And my first crop was golden
    When I brought Mary home.

Now still down Reedy River
    The grassy sheoaks sigh;
The waterholes still mirror
    The pictures in the sky;
The golden sand is drifting
    Across the rocky bars;
And over all for ever
    Go sun and moon and stars.

But of the hut I builded
    There are no traces now,
And many rains have levelled
    The furrows of my plough.
The glad bright days have vanished;
    For sombre branches wave
Their wattle-blossom golden
    Above my Mary's grave.

REEDY RIVER
Oil on hardboard 14 in. × 18 in. 1973

The Water-Lily

A lonely young wife
In her dreaming discerns
A lily-decked pool
With a border of ferns,
And a beautiful child,
With butterfly wings,
Trips down to the edge of the water and sings:
    "Come, mamma! come!
    Quick! follow me!
Step out on the leaves of the water-lily!"

And the lonely young wife,
Her heart beating wild,
Cries, "Wait till I come,
Till I reach you, my child!"
But the beautiful child
With butterfly wings
Steps out on the leaves of the lily and sings:
    "Come, mamma! come!
    Quick! follow me!
And step on the leaves of the water-lily!"

And the wife in her dreaming
Steps out on the stream,
But the lily leaves sink
And she wakes from her dream.
Ah, the waking is sad,
For the tears that it brings,
And she knows 'tis her dead baby's spirit that sings:
    "Come, mamma! come!
    Quick! follow me!
Step out on the leaves of the water-lily!"

THE WATER-LILY
Oil on hardboard 14 in. × 18 in. 1973

The Blue Mountains

ABOVE the ashes straight and tall,
  Through ferns with moisture dripping,
I climb beneath the sandstone wall,
  My feet on mosses slipping.

Like ramparts round the valley's edge
  The tinted cliffs are standing,
With many a broken wall and ledge,
  And many a rocky landing.

And round about their rugged feet
  Deep ferny dells are hidden
In shadowed depths, whence dust and heat
  Are banished and forbidden.

The stream that, crooning to itself,
  Comes down a tireless rover,
Flows calmly to the rocky shelf,
  And there leaps bravely over.

Now pouring down, now lost in spray
  When mountain breezes sally,
The water strikes the rock midway,
  And leaps into the valley.

Now in the west the colours change,
  The blue with crimson blending;
Behind the far Dividing Range
  The sun is fast descending.

And mellowed day comes o'er the place,
  And softens ragged edges;
The rising moon's great placid face
  Looks gravely o'er the ledges.

THE BLUE MOUNTAINS
Oil on hardboard 14 in. × 18 in. 1973

Taking His Chance

THEY stood by the door of the Inn on the Rise;
May Carney looked up in the bushranger's eyes:
"Oh! why did you come?—it was mad of you, Jack;
You know that the troopers are out on your track."
A laugh and a shake of his obstinate head—
"I wanted a dance, and I'll chance it," he said.

Some twenty-odd Bushmen had come to the ball,
But Jack from his youth had been known to them all,
And bushmen are soft where a woman is fair,
So the love of May Carney protected him there.
Through all the short evening—it seems like romance—
She danced with a bushranger taking his chance.

'Twas midnight—the dancers stood suddenly still,
For hoof-beats were heard on the side of the hill!
Ben Duggan, the drover, along the hillside
Came riding as only a bushman can ride.
He sprang from his horse, to the dancers he sped—
"The troopers are down in the gully!" he said.

Quite close to the shanty the troopers were seen.
"Clear out and ride hard for the ranges, Jack Dean!
Be quick!" said May Carney—her hand on her heart—
"We'll bluff them awhile, and 'twill give you a start."
He lingered a moment—to kiss her, of course—
Then ran to the trees where he'd hobbled his horse.

She ran to the gate, and the troopers were there—
The jingle of hobbles came faint on the air—
Then loudly she screamed: it was only to drown
The treacherous clatter of sliprails let down.
But troopers are sharp, and she saw at a glance
That someone was taking a desperate chance.

They chased, and they shouted, "Surrender, Jack Dean!"
They called him three times in the name of the Queen.
Then came from the darkness the clicking of locks;
The crack of a rifle was heard in the rocks!
A shriek, and a shout, and a rush of pale men—
And there lay the bushranger, chancing it then.

The sergeant dismounted and knelt on the sod—
"Your bushranging's over—make peace, Jack, with God!"
The dying man laughed—not a word he replied,
But turned to the girl who knelt down by his side.
He gazed in her eyes as she lifted his head:
"Just kiss me—my girl—and—I'll—chance it," he said.

TAKING HIS CHANCE
Oil on hardboard 14 in. × 18 in. 1973

To an Old Mate

OLD MATE! In the gusty old weather,
When our hopes and our troubles were new,
In the years spent in wearing out leather,
I found you unselfish and true—
I have gathered these verses together
For the sake of our friendship and you.

You may think for awhile, and with reason,
Though still with a kindly regret,
That I've left it full late in the season
To prove I remember you yet;
But you'll never judge me by their treason
Who profit by friends—and forget.

I remember, Old Man, I remember—
The tracks that we followed are clear—
The jovial last nights of December,
The solemn first days of the year,
Long tramps through the clearings and timber,
Short partings on platform and pier.

I can still feel the spirit that bore us,
And often the old stars will shine—
I remember the last spree in chorus
For the sake of that other Lang Syne
When the tracks lay divided before us,
Your path through the future and mine.

Through the frost-wind that cut like whip-lashes,
Through the ever-blind haze of the drought—
And in fancy at times by the flashes
Of light in the darkness of doubt—
I have followed the tent-poles and ashes
Of camps that we moved farther out.

You will find in these pages a trace of
That side of our past which was bright,
And recognize sometimes the face of
A friend who has dropped out of sight—
I send them along in the place of
The letters I promised to write.

TO AN OLD MATE
Oil on hardboard 14 in. × 18 in. 1973

On the Night Train

HAVE you seen the Bush by moonlight from the train go running by,
Here a patch of glassy water, there a glimpse of mystic sky?
Have you heard the still voice calling, yet so warm, and yet so cold:
"I'm the Mother-Bush that bore you! Come to me when you are old?"

Did you see the Bush below you sweeping darkly to the range,
All unchanged and all unchanging, yet so very old and strange!
Did you hear the Bush a-calling, when your heart was young and bold:
"I'm the Mother-Bush that nursed you! Come to me when you are old?"

Through the long, vociferous cutting as the night train swiftly sped,
Did you hear the grey Bush calling from the pine-ridge overhead:
"You have seen the seas and cities; all seems done, and all seems told;
I'm the Mother-Bush that loves you! Come to me, now you are old?"

ON THE NIGHT TRAIN
Oil on hardboard 14 in. × 18 in. 1973

Days When We Went Swimming

THE breezes waved the silver grass
    Waist-high along the siding,
And to the creek we ne'er could pass,
    Three boys, on bare back riding;
Beneath the sheoaks in the bend
    The waterhole was brimming—
Do you remember yet, old friend,
    The times we went in swimming?

The days we played the wag from school—
    Joys shared—but paid for singly—
The air was hot, the water cool—
    And naked boys are kingly!
With mud for soap, the sun to dry—
    A well-planned lie to stay us,
And dust well rubbed on neck and face
    Lest cleanliness betray us.

And you'll remember farmer Kutz—
    Though scarcely for his bounty—
He'd leased a forty-acre block,
    And thought he owned the county;
A farmer of the old-world school,
    That men grew hard and grim in,
He drew his water from the pool
    That we preferred to swim in.

And do you mind when down the creek
    His angry way he wended,
A green-hide cartwhip in his hand
    For our young backs intended?
Three naked boys upon the sand—
    Half-buried and half-sunning—
Three startled boys without their clothes
    Across the paddocks running.

We'd had some scares, but we looked blank
    When, resting there and chumming,
We glanced by chance along the bank
    And saw the farmer coming!
Some home impressions linger yet
    Of cups of sorrow brimming;
I hardly think that we'll forget
    The last day we went swimming.

DAYS WHEN WE WENT SWIMMING
Oil on hardboard 14 in. × 18 in. 1973

The Roaring Days

The night too quickly passes
   And we are growing old,
So let us fill our glasses
   And toast the Days of Gold;
When finds of wondrous treasure
   Set all the South ablaze,
And you and I were faithful mates
   All through the Roaring Days!

Then stately ships came sailing
   From every harbour's mouth,
And sought the Land of Promise
   That beaconed in the South;
Then southward streamed their streamers
   And swelled their canvas full
To speed the wildest dreamers
   E'er borne in vessel's hull.

Their shining El Dorado
   Beneath the southern skies
Was day and night for ever
   Before their eager eyes.
The brooding bush, awakened,
   Was stirred in wild unrest,
And all the year a human stream
   Went pouring to the West.

The rough bush roads re-echoed
   The bar-room's noisy din,
When troops of stalwart horsemen
   Dismounted at the inn.
And oft the hearty greetings
   And hearty clasp of hands
Would tell of sudden meetings
   of friends from other lands.

And when the cheery camp-fire
   Explored the bush with gleams,
The camping-grounds were crowded
   With caravans of teams;
Then home the jests were driven,
   And good old songs were sung,
And choruses were given
   The strength of heart and lung.

Oft when the camps were dreaming,
   And fires began to pale,
Through rugged ranges gleaming

THE ROARING DAYS
Oil on hardboard 14 in. × 18 in. 1973

Swept on the Royal Mail.
Behind six foaming horses,
    And lit by flashing lamps,
Old Cobb and Co., in royal state,
    Went dashing past the camps.

Oh, who would paint a goldfield,
    And paint the picture right,
As old Adventure saw it
    In early morning's light?
The yellow mounds of mullock
    With spots of red and white,
The scattered quartz that glistened
    Like diamonds in light;

The azure line of ridges,
    The bush of darkest green,
The little homes of calico
    That dotted all the scene.
The flat straw hats, with ribands.
    That old engravings show—
The dress that still reminds us
    Of sailors, long ago.

I hear the fall of timber
    From distant flats and fells,
The pealing of the anvils
    As clear as little bells,
The rattle of the cradle,
    The clack of windlass-boles,
The flutter of the crimson flags
    Above the golden holes.

Ah, then their hearts were bolder,
    And if Dame Fortune frowned
Their swags they'd lightly shoulder
    And tramp to other ground.
Oh, they were lion-hearted
    Who gave our country birth!
Stout sons, of stoutest fathers born,
    From all the lands on earth!

Those golden days are vanished,
    And altered is the scene;
The diggings are deserted,
    The camping-grounds are green;
The flaunting flag of progress
    Is in the West unfurled,
The mighty Bush with iron rails
    Is tethered to the world.

Grog-an'-Grumble Steeplechase

'Twixt the coastline and the border lay the town of
    Grog-an'-Grumble
  (Just two pubs beside a racecourse in a wilderness of sludge)
An' they say the local meeting was a drunken rough-and-tumble,
    Which was ended pretty often by an inquest on the judge.
Yes, 'tis said the city talent very often caught a tartar
    In the Grog-an'-Grumble sportsman, 'n' retired with
      broken heads,
For the fortune, life, and safety of the Grog-an'-Grumble starter
    Mostly hung upon the finish of the local thoroughbreds.

Pat M'Durmer was the owner of a horse they called The
    Screamer,
Which he called the "quickest shtepper 'twixt the Darling
    and the sea,"
But I think it's very doubtful if a Banshee-haunted dreamer
    Ever saw a more outrageous piece of equine scenery;
For his points were most decided, from his end to his beginning;
    He had eyes of different colour, and his legs they wasn't mates.
Pat M'Durmer said he always came "widin a flip av winnin',"
    An' his sire had come from England, 'n' his dam was from the
      States.

Friends would argue with M'Durmer, and they said he was in
    error
    To put up his horse The Screamer, for he'd lose in any case,
And they said a city racer by the name of Holy Terror
    Was regarded as the winner of the coming steeplechase;
Pat declared he had the knowledge to come in when it was raining,
    And irrelevantly mentioned that he knew the time of day,
So he rose in their opinion. It was noticed that the training
    Of The Screamer was conducted in a dark, mysterious way.

Well, the day arrived in glory; 'twas a day of jubilation
    For the careless-hearted bushmen quite a hundred miles
      around,
An' the rum 'n' beer 'n' whisky came in waggons from the
    station,
    An' the Holy Terror talent were the first upon the ground.
Judge M'Ard—with whose opinion it was scarcely safe to
    wrestle—
    Took his dangerous position on the bark-and-sapling stand:
He was what the local Stiggins used to speak of as a "wessel
    Of wrath," and he'd a bludgeon that he carried in his hand.

"Off ye go!" the starter shouted, as down fell a stupid jockey;
  Off they started in disorder—left the jockey where he lay—
And they fell and rolled and galloped down the crooked course
    and rocky,
  Till the pumping of The Screamer could be heard a mile away.
But he kept his legs and galloped; he was used to rugged
    courses,
  And he lumbered down the gully till the ridge began to quake:
And he ploughed along the sidling, raising earth till other horses
  An' their riders, too, were blinded by the dust-cloud in his
    wake.

From the ruck he'd struggle slowly—they were much surprised
    to find him
  Close abeam of Holy Terror as along the flat they tore—
Even higher still and denser rose the cloud of dust behind him,
  While in more divided splinters flew the shattered rails before.
"Terror!" "Dead heat!" they were shouting—"Terror!" but
    The Screamer hung out
  Nose to nose with Holy Terror as across the creek they swung,
An' M'Durmer shouted loudly, "Put yer tongue out, put yer
    tongue out!"
  An' The Screamer put his tongue out, and he won by
    half-a-tongue.

GROG-AN'-GRUMBLE STEEPLECHASE
Oil on hardboard 35 cm × 45 cm 1975

Here's Luck

Old Time is tramping close to-day—you hear his bluchers fall,
A mighty change is on the way, an' God protect us all;
Some dust'll fly from beery coats—at least it's been declared.
I'm glad that women has the votes—but just a trifle scared.

I'm just a trifle scared—For why? The women mean to rule;
I feel just like in days gone by when I was caned at school.
The days of men is nearly dead—of double moons and stars—
They'll soon put out our pipes, 'tis said, an' close the public bars.

No more we'll take a glass of ale to banish care an' strife,
An' chuckle home with that old tale we used to tell the wife.
We'll laugh an' joke an' sing no more with jolly beery chums,
Or shout "Here's luck!" while waitin' for the luck that never
        comes.

Did we prohibit swillin' tea—clean out of commonsense!—
Or legislate 'gainst gossipin' across a backyard fence?
Did we prohibit bustles, or the hoops when they was here?
The women never think of this—yet want to stop our beer.

The track o' life is dry enough, an' crossed with many a rut,
But, oh! we'll find it rougher still when all the pubs is shut,
When all the pubs is shut, an' closed the doors we used to seek,
An' we go toilin', thirstin' on through Sundays all the week.

For since the days when pubs was "inns"—in years gone
        past 'n' far—
Poor sinful souls have drowned their sins an' sorrows at the bar;
An' though at times it led to crime, an' debt, and such
        complaints—
Will times be happier in the days when all mankind is saints?

'Twould make the bones of Bacchus leap an' bust his coffin lid;
And Burns' ghost would wail an' weep as Robbie never did;
But let the preachers preach in style, an' rave, and rant, 'n' buck,
I rather guess they'll hear awhile the old war-cry;
        "Here's Luck!"

The world may wobble round the sun, an' all the banks go bung,
But pipes'll smoke, an' liquor run, while *Auld Lang Syne*
        is sung.
While men are driven through the mill, an' flinty times is struck,
They'll find the private entrance still!
        Here's Luck, old man—Here's Luck!

HERE'S LUCK
Oil on hardboard 35 cm × 45 cm 1975

Corny Bill

His old clay pipe stuck in his mouth,
  His hat pushed from his brow,
His dress best fitted for the South—
  I think I see him now;
And when the streets are very still,
  And sleep upon me comes,
I often dream that me an' Bill
  Are humpin' of our drums.

I mind the time when first I came
  A stranger to the land;
And I was stumped, an' sick, an' lame
  When Bill took me in hand.
And when we'd journeyed damp an' far,
  An' clouds were in the skies,
We'd camp in some old shanty bar,
  And sit a-tellin' lies.

Though time had writ upon his brow
  And rubbed away his curls,
He always was—an' may be now—
  A favourite with the girls;
I've heard bush-wimmin scream an' squall—
  I've see'd 'em laugh until
They could not do their work at all,
  Because of Corny Bill.

He was the jolliest old pup
  As ever you did see,
And often at some bush kick-up
  They'd make old Bill M.C.
He'd make them dance and sing all night,
  He'd make the music hum,
But he'd be gone at mornin' light
  A-humpin' of his drum.

Though joys of which the poet rhymes
  Was not for Bill an' me,
I think we had some good old times
  Out on the wallaby.
I took a wife and left off rum,
  An' camped beneath a roof;
But Bill preferred to hump his drum
  A-paddin' of the hoof.

"THE DREAM" FROM CORNY BILL
Oil on hardboard 35 cm × 45 cm 1975

The lazy, idle loafers wot
  In toney houses camp
Would call old Bill a drunken sot,
  A loafer, or a tramp;
But if the dead get up again—
  As preachers say they will—
I'd take my chance of judgment then
  Along of Corny Bill.

His long life's day is nearly o'er,
  Its shades begin to fall;
He soon must sling his bluey for
  The last long tramp of all;
I trust that when, in bush an' town,
  He's lived and laughed his fill,
They'll let the golden sliprails down
  For poor old Corny Bill.

CORNY BILL
Oil on hardboard 35 cm × 45 cm 1975

CUTTING CANEGRASS
Oil on hardboard 35 cm × 45 cm 1975

Paroo River

It was a week from Christmas-time,
    As near as I remember,
And half a year since, in the rear,
    We'd left the Darling Timber.
The track was hot and more than drear;
    The day dragged out for ever;
But now we knew that we were near
    Our Camp—the Paroo River.

With blighted eyes and blistered feet,
    With stomachs out of order,
Half-mad with flies and dust and heat
    We'd crossed the Queensland Border.
I longed to hear a stream go by
    And see the circles quiver;
I longed to lay me down and die
    That night on Paroo River.

The "nose-bags" heavy on each chest
    (God bless one kindly squatter!),
With grateful weight our hearts they
        pressed—
    We only wanted water.
The sun was setting in a spray
    Of colour like a liver—
We'd fondly hoped to camp and stay
    That night by Paroo River.

A cloud was on my mate's broad brow,
    And once I heard him mutter:
"What price the good old Darling, now?—
    God bless that grand old gutter!"
And then he stopped and slowly said
    In tones that made me shiver:
"It cannot well be on ahead—
    I think we've crossed the river."

But soon we saw a strip of ground
    Beside the track we followed,
No damper than the surface round,
    But just a little hollowed.
His brow assumed a thoughtful frown—
    This speech he did deliver:
"I wonder if we'd best go down
    Or up the blessed river?"

"But where," said I, " 's the blooming stream?"
   And he replied, "We're at it!"
I stood awhile, as in a dream,
   "Great Scott!" I cried, "is *that* it?
Why, that is some old bridle-track!"
   He chuckled, "Well, I never!
It's plain you've never been Out Back—
   This *is* the Paroo River!"

NEAR THE DARLING RIVER
Oil on hardboard 35 cm × 45 cm 1975

Knocking Around

Weary old wife, with the bucket and cow,
"How's your son Jack? and where is he now?"
Haggard old eyes that turn to the west—
"Boys will be boys, and he's gone with the rest!"
Grief without tears and grief without sound;
"Somewhere up-country he's knocking around."
  Knocking around with a vagabond crew,
  Does for himself what a mother would do;
  Maybe in trouble and maybe hard-up,
  Maybe in want of a bite or a sup;
  Dead of the fever, or lost in the drought,
  Lonely old mother! he's knocking about.

Wiry old man at the tail of the plough,
"Heard of Jack lately? and where is he now?"
Pauses a moment his forehead to wipe,
Drops the rope reins while he feels for his pipe,
Scratches his grey head in sorrow or doubt:
"Somewhere or other he's knocking about."
  Knocking about on the runs of the West,
  Holding his own with the worst and the best,
  Breaking in horses and risking his neck,
  Droving or shearing and making a cheque;
  Straight as a sapling—six-foot, and sound,
  Jack is all right when he's knocking around.

KNOCKING AROUND
Oil on hardboard 45 cm × 35 cm 1975

OUT BACK I Oil on hardboard 27 cm × 71 cm 1975

Out Back

The old year went, and the new returned, in the withering weeks
of drought;
The cheque was spent that the shearer earned, and the sheds
were all cut out;
The publican's words were short and few, and the publican's
looks were black—
And the time had come, as the shearer knew, to carry his swag
Out Back.

For time means tucker, and tramp you must, where the scrubs and
    plains are wide,
With seldom a track that a man can trust, or a mountain peak to
    guide;
All day long in the dust and heat—when summer is on the
    track—
With stinted stomachs and blistered feet, they carry their swags
    Out Back.

He tramped away from the shanty there, when the days were
    long and hot,
With never a soul to know or care if he died on the track or
    not.
The poor of the city have friends in woe, no matter how much
    they lack,
But only God and the swagman know how a poor man fares
    Out Back.

He begged his way on the parched Paroo and the Warrego
    tracks once more,
And lived like a dog, as the swagmen do, till the Western
    stations shore;
But men were many, and sheds were full, for work in the
    town was slack—
The traveller never got hands in wool, though he tramped for
    a year Out Back.

In stifling noons when his back was wrung by its load, and the
    air seemed dead,
And the water warmed in the bag that hung to his aching arm
    like lead.
Or in times of flood, when plains were seas and the scrubs were
    cold and black,
He ploughed in mud to his trembling knees, and paid for his
    sins Out Back.

And dirty and careless and old he wore, as his lamp of hope
    grew dim;
He tramped for years, till the swag he bore seemed part of
    himself to him.
As a bullock drags in the sandy ruts, he followed the dreary
    track,
With never a thought but to reach the huts when the sun went
    down Out Back.

It chanced one day when the north wind blew in his face like a
    furnace-breath.
He left the track for a tank he knew—'twas a shorter cut to
    death;
For the bed of the tank was hard and dry, and crossed with
    many a crack.
And, oh! it's a terrible thing to die of thirst in the scrub
    Out Back.

A drover came, but the fringe of law was eastward many a mile:
He never reported the thing he saw, for it was not worth
    his while.

OUT BACK II Oil on hardboard 35 cm × 45 cm 1975

The tanks are full, and the grass is high in the mulga off
    the track,
Where the bleaching bones of a white man lie by his mouldering
    swag Out Back.

For time means tucker, and tramp they must, where the plains
    and scrubs are wide,
With seldom a track that a man can trust, or a mountain peak
    to guide;
All day long in the flies and heat the men of the outside
    track,
With stinted stomachs and blistered feet, must carry their swags
    Out Back.

97

The Fire at Ross's Farm

The squatter saw his pastures wide
  Decrease, as one by one
The farmers moving to the west
  Selected on his run;
Selectors took the water up
  And all the black-soil round;
The best grass-land the squatter had
  Was spoilt by Ross's ground.

Now many schemes to shift old Ross
  Had racked the squatter's brains,
But Sandy had the stubborn blood
  Of Scotland in his veins;
He held the land and fenced it in,
  He cleared and ploughed the soil,
And year by year a richer crop
  Repaid him for his toil.

Between the homes for many years
  The devil left his tracks:
The squatter 'pounded Ross's stock,
  And Sandy 'pounded Black's.
A well upon the lower run
  Was filled with earth and logs,
And Black laid baits about the farm
  To poison Ross's dogs.

It was, indeed, a deadly feud
  Of class and creed and race,
So Fate supplied a Romeo
  And a Juliet in the case;
And more than once across the flats,
  Beneath the Southern Cross,
Young Robert Black was seen to ride
  With pretty Jenny Ross.

One Christmas time, when months of drought
  Had parched the western creeks,
The bush-fires started in the north
  And travelled south for weeks.
At night along the river-side
  The scene was grand and strange—
The hill-fires looked like lighted streets
  Of cities in the range.

THE FIRE AT ROSS'S FARM I
Oil on hardboard 45 cm × 35 cm 1975

The cattle-tracks between the trees
    Were like long dusky aisles,
And on a sudden breeze the fire
    Would sweep along for miles;
Like sounds of distant musketry
    It crackled through the brakes,
And o'er the flat of silver grass
    It hissed like angry snakes.

It leapt across the flowing streams
    And raced the pastures through;
It climbed the trees, and lit the boughs,
    And fierce and fiercer grew.
The bees fell stifled in the smoke
    Or perished in their hives,
And with the stock the kangaroos
    Went flying for their lives.

The sun had set on Christmas Eve,
    When through the scrub-lands wide
Young Robert Black came riding home
    As only natives ride.
He galloped to the homestead door
    And gave the first alarm:
"The fire is past the granite spur,
    And close to Ross's farm.

"Now, father, send the men at once,
    They won't be wanted here;
Poor Ross's wheat is all he has
    To pull him through the year."
"Then let it burn," the squatter said;
    "I'd like to see it done—
I'd bless the fire if it would clear
    Selectors from the run.

"Go if you will," the squatter said,
    "You shall not take the men—
Go out and join your precious friends,
    But don't come here again."
"I won't come back," young Robert cried,
    And, reckless in his ire,
He sharply turned his horse's head
    And galloped towards the fire.

THE FIRE AT ROSS'S FARM II
Oil on hardboard 35 cm × 45 cm 1975

And there for three long weary hours,
    Half-blind with smoke and heat,
Old Ross and Robert fought the flames
    That neared the ripened wheat.
The farmer's hand was nerved by fear
    Of danger and of loss;
And Robert fought the stubborn foe
    For love of Jenny Ross.

But serpent-like the curves and lines
    Slipped past them, and between
Until they reached the boundary where
    The old coach-road had been.
"The track is now our only hope,
    There we must stand," cried Ross,
"For nought on earth can stop the fire
    If once it gets across."

Then came a cruel gust of wind,
    And, with a fiendish rush,
The flames leapt o'er the narrow path
    And lit the fence of brush.
"The crop must burn!" the farmer cried,
    "We cannot save it now,"
And down upon the blackened ground
    He dashed his ragged bough.

But wildly, in a rush of hope,
    His heart began to beat,
For o'er the crackling fire he heard
    The sound of horses' feet.
"Here's help at last," young Robert cried,
    And even as he spoke
The squatter with a dozen men
    Came racing through the smoke.

Down on the ground the stockmen jumped
    And bared each brawny arm;
They tore green branches from the trees
    And fought for Ross's farm;
And when before the gallant band
    The beaten flames gave way,
Two grimy hands in friendship joined—
    And it was Christmas Day.

The Shanty on the Rise

When the caravans of wool-teams climbed the ranges from
    the West,
On a spur among the mountains stood The Bullock-drivers'
    Rest;
It was built of bark and saplings, and was rather rough
    inside,
But 'twas good enough for bushmen in the careless days
    that died—
Just a quiet little shanty kept by "Something-in-Disguise,"
As the bushmen called the landlord of the Shanty on the Rise.

City swells who "do the Royal" would have called the
    Shanty low,
But 'twas better far and cleaner than some toney pubs
    we know;
For the patrons of the Shanty had the principles of men,
And the spieler, if he struck it, wasn't welcome there again.
You could smoke and drink in quiet, yarn (or p'raps
    soliloquize)
With a decent lot of fellows in the Shanty on the Rise.

'Twas the bullock-driver's haven when his team was on
    the road,
And the waggon-wheels were groaning as they ploughed
    beneath the load;
I remember how the teamsters struggled on while it was light,
Just to camp within a cooee of the Shanty for the night;
And I think the very bullocks raised their heads and fixed
    their eyes
On the candle in the window of the Shanty on the Rise.

And the bullock-bells were clanking from the marshes on
    the flats
As we hurried to the Shanty, where we hung our dripping
    hats;
Then we took a drop of something that was brought at our
    desire,
As we stood with steaming moleskins in the kitchen by the
    fire.
Oh, it roared upon a fireplace of the good old-fashioned size,
When the rain came down the chimney of the Shanty on
    the Rise.

They got up a Christmas party in the Shanty long ago,
While we camped with Jimmy Nowlett on the river-bank below;
Poor old Jim was in his glory—they'd elected him M.C.,
For there wasn't such another raving lunatic as he.
"Mr Nowlett! Mr Swaller!" shouted Something-in-Disguise,
As we walked into the parlour of the Shanty on the Rise.

There is little real pleasure in the city where I am—
There's a "swarry" round the corner with its mockery and
        sham;
But a fellow can be happy when around the room he whirls
In a party Up-the-Country with the jolly country girls.
Why, at times I almost fancied I was dancing on the skies,
When I danced with Mary Carey in the Shanty on the Rise.

Jimmy came to me and whispered, and I muttered, "Go along!"
But he shouted "Mr Swaller will oblige us with a song!"
And at first I said I wouldn't, and I shammed a little too,
Till the girls began to whisper, "Mr Swallow, now, ah, do!"
So I sang a song of something 'bout the love that never dies,
And the chorus shook the rafters of the Shanty on the Rise.

Jimmy burst his concertina, and the bullock-drivers went
For the corpse of Joe the Fiddler, who was sleeping in his tent;
Joe was tired and had lumbago, and he wouldn't come, he said,
But the case was very urgent, so they pulled him out of bed;
And they fetched him, for the Bushmen knew that
        Something-in-Disguise
Had a cure for Joe's lumbago in the Shanty on the Rise.

Jim and I were rather quiet while escorting Mary home,
'Neath the stars that hung in clusters, near and distant,
        from the dome;
And we walked in such a silence, being lost in reverie,
That we heard the "settlers'-matches" softly rustle on the tree;
And I wondered who would win her, when she said her
        sweet good-byes—
But she died at one-and-twenty, and was buried on the Rise.

I suppose the Shanty vanished from the ranges long ago,
And the girls are mostly married to the chaps I used to know.
My old chums are in the distance—some have crossed the
        border-line,
But in fancy still their glasses chink against the rim of mine;
And, upon the very centre of the greenest spot that lies
In my fondest recollection, stands the Shanty on the Rise.

THE SHANTY ON THE RISE
Oil on hardboard 35 cm × 45 cm 1975

THE SONG AND THE SIGH Oil on hardboard 35 cm × 45 cm 1975

The Song and the Sigh

The creek went down with a broken song,
  'Neath the sheoaks high;
The waters carried the tune along,
  And the oaks a sigh.

The song and the sigh went winding by,
  Went winding down;
Circling the foot of the mountain high
  And the hillside brown.

They were hushed in the swamp of the Dead Man's Crime,
  Where the curlews cried;
But they reached the river the selfsame time,
  And there they died.

And the creek of life goes winding on,
  Wandering by;
And bears for ever, its course upon,
  A song and a sigh.

The Bush Fire

On the runs to the west of the Dingo Scrub there was drought,
      and ruin, and death,
And the sandstorm came from the dread north-east with the
      blast of a furnace-breath;
Till at last one day, at the fierce sunrise, a boundary-rider woke,
And saw in the place of the distant haze a curtain of light-blue
      smoke.

There is saddling-up by the cocky's hut, and out in the
      station yard,
And away to the north, north-east, north-west, the bushmen
      are riding hard.
The pickets are out, and many a scout, and many a mulga wire,
While Bill and Jim, their faces grim, are riding to meet the fire.

It roars for days in the trackless scrub, and across, where the
      ground seems clear,
With a crackle and rush, like the hissing of snakes, the fire
      draws near and near;
Till at last, exhausted by sleeplessness, and the terrible toil and
      heat,
The squatter is crying, "My God! the wool!" and the farmer,
      "My God! the wheat!"

But there comes a drunkard (who reels as he rides) with news
      from the roadside pub:—
"Pat Murphy—the cocky—cut off by the fire!—way back in
      the Dingo Scrub!
Let the wheat and the woolshed go to ——" Well, they do as
      each great heart bids;
They are riding a race for the Dingo Scrub—for Pat and his
      wife and kids.

And who are leading the race with Death? An ill-matched three,
      you'll allow;
Flash Jim the breaker and Boozing Bill (who is riding steadily
      now),
And Constable Dunn, of the Mounted Police, on the grey
      between the two
(He wants Flash Jim, but that job can wait till they get the
      Murphys through).

As they strike the track through the blazing scrub, the trooper is
    heard to shout:
"We'll take them on to the Two-mile Tank, if we cannot bring
    them out!"
A half-mile more, and the rest rein back, retreating,
    half-choked, half-blind;
And the three are gone from the sight of men, and the bush fire
    roars behind.

The Bushmen wiped the smoke-made tears, and like Bushmen
    laughed and swore.
"Poor Bill will be wanting his drink to-night as never he did
    before."
"And Dunn was the best in the whole damned force!"
    says a client of Dunn's, with pride;
"I reckon he'll serve his summons on Jim—when they get to the
    other side."

       .   .   .   .   .   .

It is daylight again, and the fire is past, and the black scrub
    silent and grim
Except for the blaze in an old dead tree, or the crash of a falling
    limb;
And the Bushmen are riding across the waste, with hearts and
    with eyes that fill,
To look at the bodies of Constable Dunn, Flash Jim, and
    Boozing Bill.

They are found in the mud of the Two-mile Tank, where a fiend
    might scarce survive,
But the Bushmen gather from words they hear that the bodies
    are much alive.
There is Swearing Pat, with his grey beard singed, and language
    of lurid hue,
And his tough old wife, and his half-baked kids, and the three
    who dragged them through.

THE BUSH FIRE I
Oil on hardboard 35 cm × 45 cm 1975

THE BUSH FIRE II Oil on hardboard 27 cm × 71 cm 1975

Old Pat is deploring his burnt-out home, and his wife the
     climate warm;
And Jim the loss of his favourite horse and Dunn of his
     uniform;
And Boozing Bill, with a raging thirst, is cursing the Dingo
     Scrub,
But all he'll ask is the loan of a flask and a lift to the nearest pub.

Flash Jim the Breaker is lying low—blue-paper is after Jim,
But Dunn, the trooper, is riding his rounds with a blind eye out
        for him;
And Boozing Bill is fighting D.Ts. in the township of
        Sudden Jerk—
When they're wanted again in the Dingo Scrub, they'll be there
        to do the work.

Talbragar

Jack Denver died on Talbragar when Christmas Eve began,
And there was sorrow round the place, for Denver was a man;
Jack Denver's wife bowed down her head—her daughter's
    grief was wild,
And big Ben Duggan by the bed stood sobbing like a child.
But big Ben Duggan saddled up, and galloped fast and far,
To raise the biggest funeral yet seen on Talbragar.
        By station home
        And shearing shed
        Ben Duggan cried, "Jack Denver's dead!
        Roll up at Talbragar!"

He borrowed horses here and there, and rode all Christmas Eve,
And scarcely paused a moment's time the mournful news to
    leave;
He rode by lonely huts and farms until the day was done.
And then he turned his horse's head and made for Ross's Run.
No bushman in a single day had ridden half so far
Since Johnson brought the doctor to his wife at Talbragar.
        By digger's camps
        Ben Duggan sped—
        At each he cried, "Jack Denver's dead!
        Roll up at Talbragar!"

That night he passed the humpies of the splitters on the ridge,
And roused the bullock-drivers camped at Belinfante's Bridge;
And as he climbed the ridge again the moon shone on the rise—
Did moonbeams glisten in the mist of tears that filled his eyes?
He dashed the rebel drops away—for blinding things they are—
But 'twas his best and truest friend who died on Talbragar.
        At Blackman's Run
        Before the dawn,
        Ben Duggan cried, "Jack Denver's gone!
        Roll up at Talbragar!"

At all the shanties round the place they heard his horse's tramp,
He took the track to Wilson's Luck, and told the digger's camp;
But in the gorge by Deadman's Gap the mountain shades were
    black,
And there a newly-fallen tree was lying on the track;
He saw too late—and then he heard the swift hoof's sudden jar,
And big Ben Duggan ne'er again rode home to Talbragar.
        "The wretch is drunk,
        And Denver's dead—
        A burning shame!" the people said
        Next day at Talbragar.

TALBRAGAR
Oil on hardboard 35 cm × 45 cm 1975

For thirty miles round Talbragar the boys rolled up in strength,
And Denver had a funeral a good long mile in length;
Round Denver's grave that Christmas Day rough Bushmen's
     eyes were dim—
The Western Bushmen knew the way to bury dead like him;
But some returning homeward found, by light of moon and star,
Ben Duggan lying in the rocks, five miles from Talbragar.
       And far and wide
       When Duggan died,
       The bushmen of the western side
       Rode in to Talbragar.

"DEAD DUGGAN" FROM TALBRAGAR
Oil on hardboard 45 cm × 35 cm 1975

The Old Bark School

It was built of bark and poles, and the roof was full of holes
    And each leak in rainy weather made a pool;
And the walls were mostly cracks lined with calico and sacks—
    There was little need for windows in the school.

Then we rode to school and back by the rugged gully-track,
    On the old grey horse that carried three or four;
And he looked so very wise that he lit the Master's eyes
    Every time he put his head in at the door.

(He had run with Cobb and Co.—"That grey leader, let him go!"
    There were men "as knowed the brand upon his hide,"
Some "as knowed him on the course"—Funeral service:
      "Good old horse!"
When we burnt him in the gully where he died.)

Kevin was the master's name, 'twas from Ireland that he came,
    Where the tanks are always full, and feed is grand;
And the joker then in vogue said his lessons wid a brogue—
    'Twas unconscious imitation, understand.

And we learnt the world in scraps from some ancient
      dingy maps
    Long discarded by the public-schools in town;
And as nearly every book dated back to Captain Cook
    Our geography was somewhat upside-down.

It was "in the book" and so—well, at that we'd let it go,
    For we never would believe that print could lie;
And we all learnt pretty soon that when school came out at noon
    "The sun is in the south part of the sky."

And Ireland!—*that* was known from the coast-line to Athlone,
    But little of the land that grave us birth;
Save that Captain Cook was killed (and was very likely grilled)
    And "our blacks are just the lowest race on earth."

And a woodcut, in its place, of the same degraded race,
    More like camels than the blackmen that we knew;
Jimmy Bullock, with the rest, scratched his head and gave it best;
    But he couldn't stick a bobtailed kangaroo!

Now the old bark school is gone, and the spot it stood upon
    Is a cattle-camp where curlews' cries are heard;
There's a brick school on the flat—an old schoolmate
      teaches that—
It was built when Mr Kevin was "transferred."

THE OLD BARK SCHOOL I
Oil on hardboard 35 cm × 45 cm 1975

But the old school comes again with exchanges 'cross the plain—
    With the *Out-Back Press* my fancy roams at large
When I read of passing stock, of a western mob or flock,
    With James Bullock, Grey, or Henry Dale in charge.

When I think how Jimmy went from the old bark school content,
    "Eddicated," with his packhorse after him,
Well . . . perhaps, if I were back, I would follow in his track,
    And let Kevin "finish" me as he did Jim.

THE OLD BARK SCHOOL II
Oil on hardboard 35 cm × 45 cm 1975

The Old Jimmy Woodser

The old Jimmy Woodser comes into the bar
    Unwelcomed, unnoticed, unknown,
Too old and too odd to be drunk with, by far;
So he glides to the end where the lunch-baskets are
    And they say that he tipples alone.

His frockcoat is green and the nap is no more,
    And his hat is not quite at its best;
He wears the peaked collar our grandfathers wore,
The black-ribbon tie that was legal of yore,
    And the coat buttoned over his breast.

When first he came in, for a moment I thought
    That my vision or wits were astray;
For a picture and page out of Dickens he brought—
'Twas an old file dropped in from the Chancery Court
    To the wine-vault just over the way.

But I dreamed, as he tasted his "bitter" to-night
    And the lights in the bar-room grew dim,
That the shades of the friends of that other day's light,
And of girls that were bright in our grandfathers' sight.
    Lifted shadowy glasses to him.

Then I opened the door, and the old man passed out,
    With his short, shuffling step and bowed head;
And I sighed; for I felt, as I turned me about,
An odd sense of respect—born of whisky no doubt—
    For the life that was fifty years dead.

And I thought—there are times when our memory trends
    Through the future, as 'twere, on its own—
That I, out-of-date ere my pilgrimage ends,
In a new-fashioned bar to dead loves and dead friends
    Might drink, like the old man, alone.

THE OLD JIMMY WOODSER
Oil on hardboard 35 cm × 45 cm 1975

Sweeney

It was somewhere in September, and the sun was going down,
When I came, in search of copy, to a Darling-River town;
"Come-and-Have-a-Drink" we'll call it—'tis a fitting name,
    I think—
And 'twas raining, for a wonder, up at Come-and-Have-a-Drink.

Underneath the pub veranda I was resting on a bunk
When a stranger rose before me, and he said that he was drunk;
He apologized for speaking; there was no offence, he swore;
But he somehow seemed to fancy that he'd seen my face before.

"No erfence," he said. I told him that he needn't mention it,
For I might have met him somewhere; I had travelled round a bit,
And I knew a lot of fellows in the Bush and in the streets—
But a fellow can't remember all the fellows that he meets.

Very old and thin and dirty were the garments that he wore,
Just a shirt and pair of trousers, and a boot, and nothing more;
He was wringing-wet and really in a sad and sinful plight,
And his hat was in his left hand, and a bottle in his right.

He agreed: You can't remember all the chaps you chance to meet,
And he said his name was Sweeney—people lived in Sussex-street.
He was camping in a stable, but he swore that he was right,
"Only for the blanky horses walkin' over him all night."

He'd apparently been fighting, for his face was black-and-blue,
And he looked as though the horses had been treading
    on him, too;
But an honest, genial twinkle in the eye that wasn't hurt
Seemed to hint of something better, spite of drink
    and rags and dirt.

It appeared that he mistook me for a long-lost mate of his—
One of whom I was the image, both in figure and in phiz—
(He'd have had a letter from him if the chap was livin' still,
For they'd carried swags together from the Gulf to Broken Hill).

Sweeney yarned awhile, and hinted that his folks were doing well,
And he told me that his father kept the Southern Cross Hotel;
And I wondered if his absence was regarded as a loss
When he left the elder Sweeney—landlord of the Southern Cross.

He was born in Parramatta, and he said, with humour grim,
That he'd like to see the city ere the liquor finished him,
But he couldn't raise the money. He was damned if he could think
What the Government was doing. Here he offered me a drink.

SWEENEY I
Oil on hardboard 35 cm × 45 cm 1975

I declined—'*twas* self-denial—and I lectured him on booze,
Using all the hackneyed arguments that preachers mostly use;
Things I'd heard in temperance lectures (I was young and
    rather green),
And I ended by referring to the man he might have been.

Then a wise expression struggled with the bruises on his face,
Though his argument had scarcely any bearing on the case:
"What's the good o' keepin' sober? Fellers rise and fellers fall;
What I might have been and wasn't doesn't trouble me at all."

But he couldn't stay to argue, for his beer was nearly gone.
He was glad, he said, to meet me, and he'd see me later on,
But he guessed he'd have to go and get his bottle filled again;
And he gave a lurch and vanished in the darkness and the rain.

      .   .   .   .   .   .

And of afternoons in cities, when the rain is on the land,
Visions come to me of Sweeney with his bottle in his hand,
With the stormy night behind him, and the pub veranda-post—
And I wonder why he haunts me more than any other ghost.

I suppose he's tramping somewhere where the bushmen
    carry swags,
Dragging round the western stations with his empty tucker-bags;
And I fancy that of evenings, when the track is growing dim,
What he "might have been and wasn't" comes along and
    troubles him.

SWEENEY II
Oil on hardboard 45 cm × 35 cm 1975

Andy's Return

With pannikins all rusty,
  And billy burnt and black,
And clothes all torn and dusty
  That scarcely hide his back;
With sun-cracked saddle-leather,
  And knotted green-hide rein,
His face burnt brown with weather,
  Our Andy's home again!

His unkempt hair is faded
  With sleeping in the wet,
He's looking old and jaded;
  But he is hearty yet.
With eyes sunk in their sockets—
  But merry as of yore;
With big cheques in his pockets,
  Our Andy's home once more!

Old Uncle's bright and cheerful;
  He wears a smiling face;
And Aunty's never tearful
  Now Andy's round the place.
Old Blucher barks for gladness;
  He broke his rusty chain,
And leapt in joyous madness
  When Andy came again.

With tales of flood and famine
  On distant northern tracks,
And shady yarns—"baal gammon!"
  Of dealings with the blacks,
From where the skies hang lazy
  On many a northern plain,
From regions dim and hazy
  Our Andy's home again!

His toil is nearly over;
  He'll soon enjoy his gains.
No more he'll be a drover,
  And cross the lonely plains.
Where sheoaks bend and quiver
  Far from the hot North-west,
At home by some cool river
  He means to build our nest.

ANDY'S RETURN
Oil on hardboard 35 cm × 45 cm 1975

Hawkers

Dust, dust, dust and a dog—
    Oh, the sheep-dog won't be last,
Where the long, long shadow of the old bay horse
    With the shadow of his mate is cast.
A brick-brown woman, with her brick-brown kids,
    And a man with his head half-mast,
The feed-bags hung, and the bedding slung,
    And the blackened bucket made fast
Where the tailboard clings to the tucker and things—
    So the hawker's van goes past.

HAWKERS
Oil on hardboard 35 cm × 45 cm 1975

Ballad of Mabel Clare

Ye children of the Land of Gold,
  I sing this song to you,
And if the jokes are somewhat old
  The central facts are new.
So be it sung, by hut and tent,
  Where tall the native grows;
And understand, the song is meant
  For singing through the nose.

There dwelt a hard old cockatoo
  On western hills far out,
Where everything is green and blue
  (Except, of course, in drought);
A crimson Anarchist was he—
  Held other men in scorn—
Yet preached that every man is free,
  And also "ekal born."

He lived in his ancestral hut—
  His missus wasn't there—
There was none other with him but
  His daughter, Mabel Clare.
Her eyes and hair were like the sun;
  Her foot was like a mat;
Her cheeks a trifle overdone;
  She was a democrat.

A manly independence, born
  Among the hills, she had;
She treated womankind with scorn,
  And often cursed her dad.
She hated swells and shining lights,
  For she had seen a few,
And she believed in Women's Rights
  (She mostly got 'em, too).

A stranger on the neighbouring run
  Sojourned, the squatter's guest;
He was unknown to anyone,
  But exquisitely dress'd;
He wore the latest toggery,
  The loudest thing in ties—
'Twas generally reckoned he
  Was something in disguise.

BALLAD OF MABEL CLARE I Oil on hardboard 45 cm × 35 cm 1975

Once strolling in the noontide heat
  Beneath the blinding glare,
This noble stranger chanced to meet
  The radiant Mabel Clare.
She saw at once he was a swell—
  According to her lights—
But, ah! 'tis very sad to tell,
  She met him oft of nights.

And, rambling through the moonlit gorge,
    She chatted all the while
Of Ingersoll, and Henry George,
    And Bradlaugh and Carlyle:
In short, he learned to love the girl,
    And things went on like this,
Until he said he was an Earl,
    And asked her to be his.

"Oh, say no more, Lord Kawlinee,
    Oh, say no more!" she said;
"Oh, say no more, Lord Kawlinee,
    I wish that I was dead:
My head is in an awful whirl,
    The truth I dare not tell—
I am a democratic girl,
    And cannot wed a swell!"

"O Love!" he cried, "but you forget
    That you are most unjust;
'Twas not my fault that I was set
    Within the upper crust.
Heed not the yarns the poets tell—
    O Darling, do not doubt
A simple lord can love as well
    As any rouseabout!

"For you I'll give my fortune up—
    I'd go to work for you!
I'll put the money in the cup
    And drop the title, too.
Oh, fly with me! Oh, fly with me
    Across the mountains blue!
Hoh, fly with me! *Hoh, fly with me!*"
    That very night she flew.

They took the train and journeyed down;
    Across the range they sped
Until they came to Sydney town,
    Where shortly they were wed.
(And still upon the western wild
    Admiring teamsters tell
How Mabel's father cursed his child
    For clearing with a swell.)

BALLAD OF MABEL CLARE II Oil on hardboard 35 cm × 45 cm 1975

"What ails my bird this bridal night?"
  Exclaimed Lord Kawlinee;
"What ails my own this bridal night?
  O Love, confide in me!"
"Oh now," she said, "that I am yaws
  You'll let me weep—I must—
For I've betrayed the people's caws
  And joined the upper crust."

Oh, proudly smiled his lordship then—
    His chimney-pot he floor'd;
"Look up, my love, and smile again,
    For I am not a lord!"
His eye-glass from his eye he tore,
    The dickey from his breast,
And turned and stood his bride before—
    A rouseabout, confess'd!

"Unknown I've loved you long," he said,
    "And I have loved you true—
A-shearing in a neighbour's shed
    I learned to worship you.
I do not care for place or pelf,
    For now, my love, I'm sure
That you will love me for myself
    And not because I'm poor.

"To prove your love I spent my cheque
    To buy this swell rig-out;
So fling your arms about my neck
    For I'm a rouseabout!"
At first she gave a startled cry,
    Then, safe from Care's alarms,
She sighed a soul-subduing sigh
    And sank into his arms.

He pawned the togs, and home he took
    His bride in all her charms;
The proud old cockatoo received
    The pair with open arms.
And long they lived; the faithful bride,
    The lowly rouseabout—
And if she wasn't satisfied
    She never let it out.